Critical English for Academic Purposes:
Theory, Politics, and Practice

Critical English for Academic Purposes:
Theory, Politics, and Practice

Sarah Benesch

Routledge
Taylor & Francis Group
New York   London

First published by Lawrence Erlbaum Associates, Inc., Publishers
10 Industrial Avenue
Mahwah, New Jersey 07430

Reprinted 2009 by Routledge

Routledge

270 Madison Avenue
New York, NY 10016

2 Park Square, Milton Park
Abingdon, Oxon OX14 4RN, UK

Cover design by Robert Attansio

Library of Congress Cataloging-in-Publication Data

Benesch, Sarah.
Critical English for academic purposes: theory, politics, and
practice/Sarah Benesch.
      p. cm.
      Includes bibliographical references and index.
      ISBN 0-8058-3433-8 (cloth : alk. Paper)
      ISBN 0-8058-3434-6 (pbk. : alk. Paper)
      1. English language—Study and teaching—Foreign
speakers. 2. English language—Rhetoric—Study and
teaching. 3. Critical thinking—Study and teaching. 4. Academic writing—Study and teaching. I. Title.
      PE1128.A2 B457 2001
      428'.0071—dc21   00-060981

10   9   8   7   6   5   4   3   2

TABLE OF CONTENTS

FOREWORD

English for specific purposes (ESP) has tended to be a practical affair, most interested in investigating needs, preparing teaching materials, and devising appropriate teaching methodologies. Perhaps because of the early British influences on its development, it has avoided broad questions of theory, and, as Swales (1994) suggests in his final editorial in ESP's flagship journal, *English for Specific Purposes*, articles published in that journal are "strikingly unengaged" (p. 201) by controversial issues of ideology.

ESP practice has thus remained essentially pragmatic; practitioners have interpreted their role as attempting to provide the maximum possible support in the limited time available. Although the worldwide role of English may be recognised at one level, at the day-to-day level, ESP teachers often find themselves in situations where they have to compete for timetable slots and students' attention. In these circumstances, priority has been given to discovering the expectations of the academic or professional community of which the students of the ESP class aspire to become full members and then reducing that information to teachable units taught over a specified and often limited time period.

This tendency to pragmatism was also considerably justified in the early days of the ESP movement by the need to justify its approach to those sceptical of its focus on selected specific features of the language. ESP defended its approach through the claim that it was more efficient and cost-effective than more traditional teaching approaches based on a general coverage of the language system. ESP has not, however, been unwilling to consider more ideological issues: The role of English in international publications has been much discussed (and criticised) in recent years and the burgeoning influence of social constructionism on ESP has raised important questions about its approaches to genre analysis. Indeed, the very pragmatic nature of ESP has, I believe, led to a readiness to draw on new ideas, and review its practices where necessary.

The rise of critical theory and critical approaches to discourse and to pedagogy has raised much more fundamental questions about ESP practice. Issues such as the role of English in publication and social constructionism are important but do not interrogate the fundamental tenets of ESP. These critical approaches, on the other hand, question the assumptions of traditional needs analysis and pragmatism that underpin the whole of ESP activity. ESP and, in particular, English for academic purposes (EAP) are criticised for adopting an unquestioning stance toward the departments and disciplinary practices that students encounter. The traditional mainstream EAP approach has been described as "accommodationist" (Benesch, 1993, p. 714) and it has been suggested that EAP too easily adopts the role of just fitting students into the mainstream activity of their department and into subordinate roles in the academic world. Benesch argues that needs analysis, the fundamental defining criterion of ESP, should be expanded to include *critical* needs analysis and *rights* analysis. The assumption of rights analysis is that classrooms and the various tasks (e.g., lectures, assignments, examinations) associated with following an academic course are sites of contention, or struggle, and that power is "always already there" (Foucault, 1980, cited in Benesch, 1999, p. 315). The issue of power relates to who makes the decisions about the content of the course and the nature of the teaching and assessment. Rights analysis aims to draw students' attention to issues of power and the fact that it is possible to raise questions about classes and assignments. It sees students not as apprentices who need to learn the rules of the academic game, but as participants in the academic process who can and should help shape the nature of the course and the forms of assessment.

Critical English for Academic Purposes: Theory, Politics, and Practice is an extremely welcome contribution to the debate about the future direction of ESP and EAP. Benesch is careful to restrict her discussion to EAP, but I believe that the ideas are relevant to the whole ESP movement. Whereas discussions of critical theory, critical discourse, and critical pedagogy have tended to be largely abstract, this book draws very fully and very effectively on ESP situations in New York that will be very familiar, at least to those working with non-native speakers of English studying in an English-language medium setting. This is thus likely to be a book whose ideas and practical suggestions will be readily understandable and relevant to ESP practitioners. Furthermore, the stance is not one of rejecting all current ESP practice but, rather of suggesting that ESP can carry out its stated aims more fully and raise its status within the academy by engaging with issues of power and struggle that arise in classrooms and institutions. I tend to think that many ESP teachers instinctively become anxious when it is suggested that they need to engage in struggle and understand issues of power; they are likely to be more receptive when they realise that in practice it means becoming more reflective about how ESP teaching can influence forms of teaching and assessment in the departments! In this regard, I find Benesch's discussion of the feminist perspective on critical theory, in chapter 4, and the application of that perspective to her teaching, very useful and informative.

One aspect of this book that strikes me as very effective is the way that it emphasises how ESP practice must vary from one context to another. Benesch show in chapter 5 how the EAP writing course associated with an introductory psychology course aimed to provide a balance for gender by concentrating on the topic of anorexia for one of its written assignments. This was a third aim added to the two aims set down by the English department: linking language and content learning, and enabling students to retake the university's writing assessment test. In the EAP course linked with the anthropology course, described in chapter 6, one emphasis was on helping students to negotiate the requirements for assignments. When the demands became excessive, in the view of the students, they were helped in the EAP class to frame appropriate requests and questions and, eventually, to form a delegation to the anthropology professor asking for a more manageable workload. In another description of a particular context, an EAP writing course linked with a different psychology course, Benesch (1999a) shows how students were helped to devise and ask the psychology professor, in actual class time, relevant questions that helped clarify points he was making in his lectures.

Each situation presented particular problems and in each case a different solution is devised.

This approach reminds me of my own work in team teaching with subject specialists (reported on in various publications, notably Dudley-Evans & St. John, 1998). In those situations, the close collaboration with the subject specialist, and the three-way interaction between the students, the subject lecturer, and the language teacher, in the actual sessions, dealt with particular problems that students had been encountering in following a lecture or carrying out an assignment. The course was thus responsive to the immediate problems that students faced at a specific time. It was, however, our belief that we, as language teachers, should act as *facilitators*, commenting on and elucidating the communication between the subject lecturer and the students. We saw our role as that of a mediator between the two sides and specifically did not comment directly on the lecturing style or the phrasing of questions when dealing with examination answers, even though the lecturers often asked us to do so. We have argued that to do so would imperil the close relationship and feeling of trust that we believe are necessary for a team teaching approach. Our judgment was probably right for a setting where language and subject teachers work together in the same classroom, but I now recognise that we may be losing certain opportunities that come in the linked class where the subject lecturer does not actually attend the EAP class. That is the opportunity to look critically at the course, and to help students develop solutions for improving problematic aspects. Certainly over the years, with the growth of the relationships from the team-taught classes, subject lecturers have increasingly sought our advise about different aspects of their master's courses or problems with their research students. And the number of problem cases being dealt with by the academic advisor to international students has increased considerably, especially in the area of difficulty between the thesis supervisor and the student. All of this indicates that there is room within the British EAP model to take the role of developing awareness among students of the expectations of the department a stage further by focusing not only on needs analysis but also on rights.

EAP has fluctuated in its relatively short history between a more general approach and more specific approaches. The more general approach has concentrated on features of language, genre, and discourse that are common to all disciplines or, at least, to broad areas of academic study, such as science, or engineering, or social science. The more specific approach has assumed that the differences between disciplines are so important that they should be the focus of EAP study. Benesch's approach clearly falls into the more specific category and she is at pains to take context into account and not to make generalisations that should apply in other EAP situations. Her position is thus consistent with the recent movement in the direction of more specific approaches to EAP. Findings in genre analysis and, in particular, the broader approach to text influenced by social constructionism, for example, have shown that texts vary considerably across disciplines and that a generalised genre approach may be limited in value.

I do not, however, wish to imply that Benesch's contribution to ESP discussion is essentially not that different from mainstream approaches. On the contrary, it represents an important and radical departure. I particularly welcome in the discussion of Freire's writings the emphasis on *hope* and *optimism* about students. It is often assumed that international students in English medium situations just want to succeed in their course or research and are not, therefore, concerned with raising questions about the teaching or the assignments, or more generally, about the quality of their academic experience. Such views may well represent an underestimation of students and their potential, even a lack of respect for their abilities. Similarly, the notion that international students may feel uncomfortable with certain Western styles of learning and that institutions may need to adapt to take account of the differences raises all sorts of interesting issues. Mainstream EAP has sometimes seemed to accept the "limitations" of international students too readily. Rights analysis, flexibly applied, would seem to offer a way of negotiating how much and what kind of adaptation to Western learning styles is and should be expected.

I have stressed the fact that Benesch's ideas arise from rich and varied teaching experiences. All that experience has been in a particular setting (i.e., a publicly funded urban college in the United States), one with parallels in the United Kingdom, Australia, and New Zealand, first world countries with large numbers of immigrant students in tertiary institutions, at the undergraduate level. It has been noted elsewhere that these situations are different from other EAP situations, even in countries whose universities are English medium, such as Hong Kong or Zimbabwe. Certainly they are different from the EAP situation in English as a foreign language countries, such as Spain, the countries of Latin America, or continental Europe, where the medium of instruction is usually the students' first language and English is very much the auxiliary language, however important. It could be argued that an approach to EAP based on the interplay between needs and rights analysis is less relevant in these kinds of situations. However, even though Benesch downplays the transferability of her experiments in critical EAP, the final chapter on the ethics of EAP is surely applicable to all settings. EAP teachers and their students have, as a result of their consideration of the discourse of their subject, much to offer to discussions about the improvement of curricula and communication about the subject.

—Tony Dudley-Evans
The University of Birmingham, UK

PREFACE

Critical English for Academic Purposes: Theory, Politics, and Practice combines two fields that have much to offer each other: English for academic purposes (EAP) and critical pedagogy. EAP grounds English language teaching in the cognitive and linguistic demands of academic target situations, tailoring instruction to specific rather than general purposes. It therefore provides informed and focused instruction, based on needs analysis. Critical pedagogy, on the other hand, is concerned with institutional power relations, studying how students' and teachers' multiple identities complicate teaching and learning. It seeks ways to democratize societies by engaging students in decisions affecting their lives in and out of school. It questions the status quo: Why are things they way they are? Who decides? What are other possibilities?

Although EAP attends to the social construction of knowledge, it has, for the most part, overlooked sociopolitical issues affecting life in and outside of academic settings. The goal has been to study how academic discourse communities construct their tasks and genres, so they can be taught more effectively to EAP students. Yet, calls for greater attention to the wider social context have been made by Dudley-Evans and St. John (1998), Master (1998), and Swales (1994) to move EAP beyond its traditional pragmatic orientation. By merging EAP and critical pedagogy, *Critical English for Academic Purposes: Theory, Politics, and Practice* answers that call. It outlines the theories of EAP and critical pedagogy, discusses their relationship in critical EAP, and offers examples of experiments in critical EAP in linked general education undergraduate courses at a U.S. college.

Critical EAP engages students in the types of activities they are asked to carry out in academic classes while encouraging them to question and, in some cases, transform those activities as well as the conditions from which they arose. It takes into account the challenges non-native English speakers (NNES) face in their content classes while viewing students as active participants who can help shape academic goals and assignments rather than passively carrying them out. By encouraging students to consciously engage in academic life, critical EAP aims to increase their participation in the workplace, civic life and other areas.

BACKGROUND

In 1985, I was hired as an assistant professor of English at the College of Staten Island (CSI), the City University of New York (CUNY). English department faculty had begun offering linked courses in 1981 at the college, as a way to provide contextualized language instruction to open admissions students. I was fortunate to be invited to teach linked courses during my first semester at CSI. It was an exciting and challenging collaboration with my colleagues, Professor Margery Cornwell and Professor Ivan Smodlaka (Benesch, 1988).

That early positive experience with linked courses led me to the literature on paired and adjunct courses, including content-based instruction and English for academic purposes. Initially, I was pleased to discover that such literatures existed. However, the publications revealed that EAP faculty were positioned, for the most part, in a service role in the paired courses they taught. They seemed mainly to subordinate their instruction to the demands of the content course to which they were joined. This was different from my experience at the College of Staten Island where the linked courses, in the Freshman Workshop Program directed by Professor Rose Ortiz, were highly collaborative with language and content teachers working together to develop curricula based on their varied areas of expertise (Benesch, 1992). Having been trained in language-across-the-curriculum methods (LAC), such as journals and peer group collaboration, as a graduate student at New York University, I was disappointed that EAP advocates were more focused on skills-based teaching than on introducing these activities in content classes, as LAC had done (Britton, Burgess, Martin, McLeod, & Rosen, 1975; Mayher, Lester, & Pradl, 1983; Torbe & Medway, 1981). They mainly accommodated their instruction to content demands rather than positioning themselves as reformers who could help improve teaching across the disciplines. If the content class relied on lecturing, EAP taught listening and note-taking skills. If the lectures were too difficult for students to understand, the EAP teachers rewrote them to enhance their comprehensibility.

These limitations in the EAP literature coupled with the changing political climate in CUNY were catalysts for considering a critical approach to EAP. In CUNY, open admissions was being dismantled through removal of credit from ESL courses, more pre requisites for mainstream courses, tuition increases, and cuts in financial aid. These dramatic changes were occurring with little faculty or student consultation. In fact, many students were unaware of new regulations until they found themselves directly affected by them. An EAP pedagogy responding only to the demands of content courses was inadequate in this climate. Therefore, I sought to join EAP and critical pedagogy to connect the world outside the classroom to the academic course work inside. This book discusses the theory, politics, and teaching of critical EAP, an experiment I have been carrying out since 1990. Critical EAP is informed by the work of various theorists, including Freire, Foucault, and feminist critical theorists such as Luke and Gore. These influences are discussed in chapter 4, and their contribution to critical EAP practice is revealed in chapters 5, 6, 7, and 8 where the theory is applied to teaching examples. A few of the theoretical underpinnings of critical EAP are briefly discussed here.

THEORETICAL UNDERPINNINGS

Problematizing Assumptions

Common to all critical approaches is interrogating assumptions on which theory and practice are based. This means questioning, or problematizing, what had been previously taken for granted, terms like "English." For example, in English for academic purposes, which English is being referred to? If academic English is not monolithic, whose gets taught? In EAP, what is "academic"? And what are the purposes? Are students' purposes congruent with those of academic institutions? If not, how can the relationship between them be theorized?

These types of questions are what Pennycook (1999) calls "critical theory as problematizing practice" (p. 341), the inclination to turn "a skeptical eye towards assumptions, ideas that have become naturalized" (p. 343). Throughout the book, I have tried to question not only the normative assumptions of EAP but also of critical pedagogy, including my own practice. One lesson of carrying out this type of interrogation is that context must be taken into account, to avoid claims and generalizations that may not hold up when applied to situations outside the one in which they were generated. The teaching examples in Part II of the book should, therefore, be seen as attempts to enact critical theory in practice rather than as transferable prototypes. They raise questions about topic choice, classroom dynamics, power relations, the role of a critical EAP teacher, and so on, rather than offering answers or making claims about what works. The pedagogical decisions discussed in those chapters were made in a particular institution with a particular group of students during a specific moment of the college's history and should be seen in that light.

Needs Analysis and Rights Analysis

The overarching goal of critical EAP is to help students perform well in their academic courses while encouraging them to question and shape the education they are being offered. It is both pragmatic and critical, grounded in the demands students face but open to the possibility of changing them. The interplay between stability and change is theorized through the relationship between needs analysis and rights analysis. *Needs analysis* is critical EAP's method for collecting data about target requirements, as it is in traditional EAP. *Rights analysis* is critical EAP's framework for studying power relations, building community, organizing students, and bringing about greater equality between language and content teachers.

Hope

Paulo Freire's influence permeates this book, particularly the notion of hope as a theoretical construct in critical pedagogy. Hope sustains a vision of what could be, offering alternatives to what already is. According to Freire (1994), teaching that simply perpetuates the status quo without the possibility of changing current conditions is training, not education:

> . . . whenever the future is considered as a pregiven—whether this be the pure, mechanical repetition of the present, or simply it 'is what it has to be'—there is no room for utopia nor therefore for the dream, the option, the decision, or expectancy in the struggle, which is the only way hope exists. There is no room for education. Only for training. (p. 91)

The struggle Freire refers to is for social justice: "for a different, less-ugly 'world'" (p. 91). Yet, the EAP literature often portrays teachers as trainers who accept and enact predetermined requirements, rather than as educators imagining a more equitable and democratic world with their students. They are expected to help students fulfill target demands unquestioningly. Hope as a construct offers a vision of EAP as the means for greater dialogue in academic classes, more interesting readings, better-conceived assignments, and greater joy in learning. It encourages students to aim for these reforms in academic institutions and then to improve conditions in the workplace and community. This is the dream of critical EAP.

COMPLEXITIES OF PRACTICE

The examples of critical EAP in Part II of the book are intended to show theory applied to teaching in particular settings. They are, in part, a response to teachers' questions about how to apply critical theory to their own practice. They discuss experiments carried out in critical EAP in two publicly funded colleges in the U.S. whose conditions and politics helped shaped curricular and pedagogical choices in the EAP and content courses. The students who happened to enroll in those courses also shaped classroom dynamics and possibilities. Therefore the examples should not be seen as enactments of a method to be tried in other settings. Although the theory of critical EAP, discussed in Part I, might inform others' experiments, each class will be different, as the classes discussed in Part II of this book differed.

Despite the risk of implying a method of critical EAP in presenting examples, I believe the benefits of illustrating theory outweigh that risk. Without descriptions of classroom experiments, theory remains a static and hollow set of principles, untested in actual settings. Trying to do critical EAP in various linked classes allowed me to understand its limits and possibilities. Students have guided the practice, a complex, ambiguous, and often exciting process. The examples in Part II are intended to capture the complexity of critical EAP practice, including the challenges of self-reflection. They are meant as encouragements to experiment with critical EAP in different contexts.

STRUCTURE AND CONTENTS OF THE BOOK

Part I of *Critical English for Academic Purposes: Theory, Politics, and Practice* focuses on the official and unofficial histories of EAP, debates about EAP pedagogy and politics, and a theory of critical EAP. Chapter 1 is an overview of the history of English for specific purposes (ESP) and a tribute to the contributions of those who established the field and have been working in it for the last 30 years. It demonstrates that ESP and EAP are vibrant fields whose aims and methods have been revised continually to offer students the best possible instruction. Chapter 2 outlines the political and economic roots of EAP, the unofficial history not usually discussed in the literature. Chapter 3 discusses EAP from the perspective of those who have raised concerns about its goals and pedagogy. Included in this chapter is the critique of L2 compositionists who argue for English for general purposes and of critical theorists whose concerns are ideological. EAP's quietism about the politics of language instruction is also highlighted, setting the stage for chapter 4, a discussion of a theory of critical EAP. In this chapter, the influences of Freire, Foucault, and feminist theorists on the following principles of critical EAP, are featured: hope; dialogue; power and resistance; rights analysis; community-building; negotiating the curriculum; and organizing. These features of critical EAP are responses to and, in some cases, alternatives to pragmatism, accommodation, individualism, and competition.

Part II of *Critical English for Academic Purposes: Theory, Politics, and Practice* applies critical EAP theory to teaching, offering examples from linked courses I have taught over 10 years. Each chapter features a different aspect of the theory. Chapter 5 takes up the allegation that critical pedagogy attempts to indoctrinate students to a particular way of thinking by revisiting my choice to teach about anorexia in a paired EAP/psychology course I had written about previously (Benesch, 1998). It problematizes that choice, demonstrating that critical pedagogy is neither indoctrination nor orthodoxy but a self-reflective undertaking that must question its assumptions and practices. Chapter 6 looks at community-building in a paired EAP/anthropology course as a political and pedagogical response to attempts to sort and segregate immigrant and international students in U.S. universities. It shows changes brought about when students organized themselves to raise questions about content course assignments.

Chapter 7 gives an example of rights analysis in a paired EAP writing/psychology lecture course where students' proposals for more time for discussion in the lecture class were met with an invitation by the psychology professor to ask questions whenever they wanted. Yet, when students asked questions, there was less time for introducing new material, revealing a conflict between dialogue and coverage in academic classes. Chapter 8 continues to problematize coverage by looking at a single assignment negotiated between three teachers and their students in a blocked EAP reading/EAP writing/social sciences course. Although the assignment was successfully negotiated, questions about coverage and the role of critical EAP in challenging that tradition remained. The conclusion, chapter 9, suggests implications for practice of the three intended audiences of this book: EAP teachers, content teachers, and critical teachers. Included in this chapter is the idea of an ethics of critical EAP.

ACKNOWLEDGMENTS

When I first began presenting my ideas about critical EAP at conferences and in writing, I wondered how the work would be received by those who had established and developed ESP and EAP. My concerns were unfounded; the reception was welcoming and open-minded. In particular, I would like to acknowledge Tony Dudley-Evans and Ann Johns for inviting me to present with them at various conferences and for encouraging my work. In addition, Tony graciously accepted my request to write the book's foreword.

Students are the reason ESL teachers find their work so gratifying. Over the years that I have participated in linked courses, students have taught me much about hope and persistence, as they struggled to balance numerous academic and personal demands: attending classes, maintaining one or more jobs, taking care of families, and studying. Two in particular have remained in touch with me over many years, and I would therefore like to acknowledge their influence on me. Dr. Won Sohn, a former EAP student in the first linked course I taught at the College of Staten Island is now a gastroenterologist practicing at Methodist Hospital in New York. As a recent arrival from Korea, he failed the reading and writing proficiency tests on entry to CUNY and was therefore placed in a linked ESL reading/writing/social sciences course. Four years later, he graduated as valedictorian of his class. He went on to medical school, including a residency at Yale University. Ruth Herzlinger, after graduating from the College of Staten Island, went on to become an early childhood special education teacher; she is also a fine painter. Both of these students are open admissions success stories. In addition, I thank the students I taught from 1992 to 1999 who appear anonymously in this book. Their written and spoken feedback has guided me and informed my understanding of critical theory and practice.

The conversations I have had with colleagues in New York and elsewhere have also provided inspiration. For these talks about teaching, learning, language, identity, and power I thank Trudy Smoke, Kate Garretson, Nancy Lester, Stephanie Vandrick, Brian Morgan, Milena Savova, Sue Starfield, Ryuko Kubota, Suresh Canagarajah, Bonny Norton, Alistair Pennycook, Ruth Spack, Vivian Zamel, Bill Johnston and Dwight Atkinson. Thanks also to Howard Kleinman and Mary O'Riordan for helping me interpret the CUNY Board of Trustees' resolution regarding ESL students.

The English department at the College of Staten Island, my professional home for the last 14 years, has been a wonderful place to grow as a teacher and scholar. I thank my colleagues Rose Ortiz, David Falk, Margery Cornwell, Maryanne Feola, Gail Wood, Peter Miller, Bill Bernhardt, and Arnold Kantrowitz for pioneering linked courses long before they became popular. I also thank Rose and David for inviting me to teach in the Freshman Workshop Program during my first semester at the college and many additional semesters thereafter.

I am grateful to CSI President Marlene Springer for granting me a sabbatical leave during the 1999–2000 academic year so that I could write this book. And thanks to Linda Roccos, of the CSI Library who so helpfully got permission for me to visit other university libraries in the New York area.

Ilona Leki and Brian Morgan were my reviewers. Not only did they read the entire first draft of the manuscript in a month, but also offered generous and intelligent feedback. Each pointed out areas to clarify and elaborate, helping me to refine the chapters. Thanks also to Dawn Lee Wakefield for her careful and thoughtful copyediting.

I met Naomi Silverman at TESOL 1996 in Chicago, but felt as if I had known her for many years. We began a conversation about education and politics that continues to this day. I cannot imagine a more supportive and intellectually engaged editor. She understood what I wanted to do, encouraged me to do it, and made sure I kept on track.

The members of my family, my sisters Jane and Amy, and my parents, Joan and Bill, have also encouraged me throughout the writing of this book.

My partner, Robert Attanasio, a talented video artist, has supported me in every way. He offered insightful comments about the manuscript, cheered me on, and provided needed distraction. His extraordinary eye brings beauty to all he does, including suggestions for this book's cover.

—Sarah Benesch

PART I:

THEORY AND POLITICS

Chapter 1

A History of English for Academic Purposes

This history of English for academic purposes (EAP), like all overviews, is subjective. Choices of which citations to include and leave out depend on the aims and predispositions of the overview's author. Yet, while acknowledging my subjectivity, in this chapter I try to present the history of EAP from the perspective of specialists who have shaped the field over the last 30 years and to honor their contributions. Further on, I highlight concerns raised about EAP from outside the field (see chap. 3). This is not to say that EAP has developed without criticism from within. On the contrary, theoretical and pedagogical differences, many of which I discuss in this chapter, are prevalent in the EAP literature as they are in all academic fields. Indeed, discussion of these conflicts has contributed to shifts in EAP's research and teaching methods over the years.

Although such contestation and debate appear frequently in the EAP literature, its politics remain largely hidden. Power issues have been ignored in the name of pragmatism, that is, fulfilling target expectations without questioning the inequities they might perpetuate or engender (Benesch, 1993). These questions, though, are not the focus of the present chapter. Instead, I save them for the next chapter in order to first present a chronology of the intellectual history of EAP, a discussion of its theoretical influences from the 1960s to the present. One way my subjectivity manifests itself in this presentation is that I devote more space to the recent years of EAP, that is, to needs analysis, study skills, linked courses and genre analysis, and less space to the early years of register analysis and rhetorical analysis. This choice was guided by my teaching and research experience, based on more recent developments in EAP's history than on earlier ones.

Some of those I cite in this overview, such as Tony Dudley-Evans, Ann Johns, and John Swales, have both participated in and chronicled EAP's history, offering a longitudinal view as well as eyewitness accounts of EAP curriculum development in particular settings. Others I cite contributed to the field during a single period, yet their work has led to refinements in EAP theory and practice.

THEORETICAL INFLUENCES

The theoretical influences that have shaped EAP throughout its 30-year history include: linguistics; applied linguistics; sociolinguistics; communicative language teaching; writing across the curriculum; learning theory; and genre studies. The emphasis, however, has been less on research and theory than on curriculum and instruction, leading some EAP specialists to raise concerns about unquestioned assumptions driving the development of classroom materials and activities. McDonough (1986), for example, is troubled that "insufficient attention is paid to the research sources from which pedagogical decisions—about materials, methodology and so on—either are drawn or might profitably be so" (p. 17). She calls for "classroom-initiated research" informed by theory to arrive at an "integrated view of research" that erases distinctions between practitioners and researchers of EAP. (p. 23) As I show in the later stages of this chronology, that type of research is currently being carried out, especially in linked courses.

Yet, there has been a positive dimension to EAP's historical favoring of application and teaching materials over research and theory. Due to its preoccupation with syllabus design, materials development, and pedagogy, EAP has become increasingly responsive to the complexities of institutions, teaching, and learning in local contexts. That is, although the early years of EAP focused mainly on teaching the lexical items and types of texts students might encounter in their work or academic courses, in recent years, social context, with its unpredictability and multiple meanings, has become a central concern. It is now recognized that knowledge is socially constructed and that linguistic analyses of texts, the basis of early EAP instruction, are an insufficient foundation of instruction. The following retrospective reveals how EAP arrived at its current acknowledgment of the centrality of context as it moved through various stages of its history: register analysis; rhetorical analysis; study skills and needs analysis; and genre analysis. These stages are presented chronologically, but it should be noted that they are overlapping and not mutually exclusive; although some EAP specialists are conducting the type of integrated classroom-based research McDonough (1986) has called for, others continue to carry out more traditional text and discourse analysis.

HISTORICAL TRENDS

Register Analysis

The early history of EAP spans the mid-1960s to the early 1970s, beginning with the emergence of English for science and technology (EST). EST, at that time, was intended to provide an alternative to English language teaching as humanities, preparing students to read literary texts. The goal was to move away from "language teaching as a handmaiden of literary studies" toward "the notion that the teaching of language can with advantage be deliberately matched to the specific needs and purposes of the learner" (Strevens, 1977, p. 89). Strevens (1971b) argued that by teaching only literature and not other kinds of texts, secondary school English teachers, in the United Kingdom and other countries, were neglecting to prepare "scientifically inclined" students for further studies. He claimed that many teachers trained in literature were predisposed to viewing science as "cold" and literature as "warm": "Literature is held to be the only morally and aesthetically worthwhile subject. Scientists are stated to be philistines . . . and any activity that smacks of measurement or quantification is low-valued" (p. 8). Reacting against what he saw as the literary bias of English language teaching, Strevens recommended offering courses geared to the eventual uses students would make of the language in their future studies and jobs. He believed that at the beginning levels, these courses might include scientific vocabulary exercises and scenarios set in scientific situations, such as labs. At more advanced levels, EST might include replicating and discussing experiments and teaching scientific texts.

The postwar boom in funding for science and technology by the United States and the United Kingdom included subsidies for English language teaching (ELT) and teacher training (in chap. 2, I explore the economic roots of EAP and their political implications). The response of ELT specialists was to shift instruction away from the traditional focus on grammar and literature toward greater attention to features of scientific English. Attempting to capture and characterize the uniqueness of scientific English, EST research during this period consisted primarily of frequency studies of lexical items and grammatical features in scientific texts. Huddlestone (1971), for example, carried out a 4-year linguistic study of 135,000 words of scientific English, looking for patterns in single sentences and clauses (cited in Macmillan, 1971a). This register analysis and similar ones were the basis of EST instruction for students who had usually acquired a degree of proficiency in reading English.

EST textbooks based on register analysis were published during this period, one example being Ewer and Latorre's *A Course in Basic Scientific English* (1969). The authors based the material on a study of 3,000,000 words of "modern scientific English ranging from popular writings to learned articles and graded according to both frequency and complexity" (Macmillan, 1971b, p. 23). Each unit of the text includes a reading passage written by the authors, comprehension questions, vocabulary exercises, structural exercises, and a discussion and criticism section. Also included are a dictionary of scientific terms and an index of grammatical structures found in the reading passages (Macmillan, 1971b).

Swales (1988) cites Herbert's (1965) EST text, *The Structure of Technical English,* as perhaps the first English for specific purposes (ESP) textbook, one based on "a serious and detached investigation into the characteristics and the language found in science and engineering written texts" (p. 17). Each section of that textbook begins with a 500-word passage written by Herbert to illustrate certain aspects of technical style rather than to convey content. The accompanying exercises serve to highlight and review lexical items and grammatical points in the passage.

EST texts of this period were admired for their "coverage of . . . semi-technical language" (Dudley-Evans & St. John, 1998, p. 21). However, they were also found to be pedagogically and theoretically unsound: "The passages were dense and lacked authenticity, the accompanying diagrams were not very supportive, and worst of all, the exercises were repetitive . . ." (p. 22). Doubts about the application of register analysis to teaching English for science and technology led EAP research away from linguistic form toward communicative purpose and role, through the use of rhetorical analysis (Robinson, 1980). Yet, Robinson (1980) acknowledges a place for register analysis in local settings: "ESP courses should be designed locally for specific target audiences with any register analysis confined to the particular set of textbooks for their special subject that a particular class employs" (p. 19). As Dudley-Evans and St. John (1998) point out, although register analysis is no longer the focal point of EAP research and teaching, the use of computers has led to a resurgent interest in quantifying grammatical features of ESP texts.

Rhetorical Analysis

The second stage of EAP, during the 1970s, was more rhetorical in focus. Rather than simply enumerating and describing linguistic features of scientific English, researchers investigated the relationship between grammatical choices and rhetorical purpose. The Washington State ESP group is usually cited as an example of discourse analysis during this period, especially its identification of levels of abstraction and rhetorical functions in scientific texts. Whereas register analysis dwelled on the grammar of sentences, this group attended to paragraphs. Hoping to help engineering students "manipulate scientific and technical information" (p. 128), Lackstrom, Selinker, and Trimble (1973), members of the Washington State group, studied two areas of grammar that their students struggled with: articles and tense choice. In particular, they focused on how presuppositions, "information shared by the technical writer and reader," affect surface-level syntactic choices of articles and tenses within paragraphs. They were not as much interested in "physical paragraphs," groups of sentences demarcated by indentation, as they were in "conceptual" ones, "organizationally- or rhetorically- related concepts which develop a given generalization in such a way as to form a coherent and complete unit of discourse" (p. 130).

To explain how concepts within a paragraph (defined in this way) interrelated, they offer a *rhetorical–grammatical process chart* for EST of four discourse levels with different rhetorical purposes but related hierarchically to each other. In the chart, the four rhetorical levels, A–D, are: purpose of the total discourse; function of the units that develop the purposes of Level A; rhetorical devices employed to develop the functions of Level B; and relational rhetorical principles that provide cohesion with the units of Level C. Level A includes presenting information, presenting a proposal, and detailing an experiment. Level B includes reporting past research, discussing theory, and stating the problem. Level C includes definition, classification, and explanation. Level D includes natural principles, such as time and space order, and logical principles, such as analogy and exemplificiation. In addition, for each level the authors include grammatical choices, articles, and tenses.

The *rhetorical–grammatical process* chart describes EST paragraph development as a set of hierarchical relationships constraining and guiding rhetorical choices. Building on this type of rhetorical analysis, Selinker, Todd-Trimble, and Trimble (1978), discuss a second method of paragraph development, *rhetorical function–shift development*. Whereas in the first type of paragraph development, generalizations and supporting statements are clearly stated, in the second type "clearly stated core ideas are seldom found" (p. 314). In addition, shifts in these paragraphs from one rhetorical function to another are not signaled, making comprehension difficult for students, according to Selinker, Todd-Trimble, and Trimble (1978). To improve the comprehension of EST texts, they taught students to anticipate shifts by carrying out rhetorical analysis, sensitizing them to changes in communicative purpose occurring in paragraphs.

Drobnic (1978) offers an example of rhetorical analysis applied to teaching materials in his discussion of a course for Taiwanese nuclear engineers. To introduce the relationship between physical and conceptual paragraphs, he first gave students a three-paragraph text on atomic fuel published by the U.S. government. The text defines atomic fuel and discusses the ingredients used to produce it. After reading the text, students completed fill-in-the-blank questions about each physical paragraph and then constructed a flowchart of all the information in the text.[1] According to

---

[1]This is one of the more dramatic examples of attention to rhetoric but not to content. Drobnic (1978) makes no mention of discussing the ethics of producing atomic fuel with the students.

Drobnic, the flowchart allowed students to grasp "the conceptual unity of the stretch of text" and to become "adept at recognizing conceptual paragraphs" (p. 11) in subsequent lessons.

Other classroom materials based on rhetorical analysis include the *English in Focus* series, edited by Patrick Allen and Henry Widdowson between 1974 and 1980, nine textbooks, each dealing with a different subject area, including medical science, agriculture, and social science. In their introduction to the teacher's edition of *English in the physical sciences,* Allen and Widdowson (1974), explain that their goal is "not to teach more grammar, but to show students how to use the grammar they already know" (p. xi). That is, the authors assume that students "have a considerable dormant competence in English" as well as "knowledge of basic science" (p. xi). The aim of the textbook, therefore, is not to teach science per se but, rather, "to develop in the reader an understanding of how this subject-matter is expressed through English" (pp. xi–xii). To carry out this goal, the authors offer eight units, seven of which open with a short simple reading passage, followed by exercises referring back to rhetorical features in the passage. The units also include guided paragraph writing and a longer reading passage intended to "approximate the kind of language that the student will find in his scientific textbooks" (p. xii).

However, assumptions on which the *English in Focus* series was based have been questioned. Robinson (1980), for example, challenges Widdowson's hypotheses that the deep cognitive structures of the sciences exist independently of their realizations in various languages and that students draw on their prior acquisition of those deep structures when learning the surface forms of scientific English. According to Robinson (1980), this formulation assumes that knowledge is separate from language and that with input from EST teachers, students can call on a storehouse of nonlinguistic scientific knowledge when learning the surface forms in the target language, a dubious and untested hypothesis, also questioned by Swales (1988). Knowledge is socially constructed, not universal or nonlinguistic, according to Swales. It is "influenced by national, social, cultural, technical, educational, and religious expectations and inspirations" (p. 72). Nor can the prior teaching of scientific knowledge in L1 be assumed, Swales points out, further calling the rationale of the *English in Focus* series into question.

Starfield's (1990) discovery that the Allen and Widdowson textbooks were not applicable to her teaching situation at the University of the Witswatersrand, South Africa supports Swales' (1998) critique of the series. Finding that her non-native speaking students had not been taught science in L1 in high school, she was forced to reject what she calls the *Widdowsonian translation approach*: "based on 'translating' into English the knowledge the students is already presumed to have in the L1" (p. 87). Her university students had been taught science in L2 by high school teachers who were themselves non-native speakers of English and who were found to be proficient neither in English nor in science. Therefore, "few assumptions can be made about students' scientific knowledge or their language proficiency" (p. 87). In place of the *translation approach*, Starfield organized team-teaching, where language and subject specialists planned and cotaught courses, thereby "embed[ding] language in the reality of students' mainstream course content" and "reducing cognitive demands on them" (p. 88). Other examples of team-teaching and linked courses, aiming to contextualize language teaching, are discussed later in this chapter.

Study Skills and Needs Analysis

Increased attention to how students acquire English in academic settings shifted emphasis from linguistic and rhetorical forms to study skills and strategies. In fact, the interest in study skills was so great that by the late 1980s, Jordan (1989) declares: "Study skills is seen as the key component of EAP" (p. 151). Coinciding with this development was the appearance of needs analyses describing the types of tasks, skills, and behaviors required of learners in present and future target situations. Munby's (1978) taxonomy of skills and functions and Richterich and Chancerel's (1977) systems approach, sponsored by the Council of Europe, are needs-analysis prototypes from that period. Jordan (1997) classifies Munby's approach as "target situation analysis," concentrating on precourse assessment of the skills required in future courses. The Council of Europe's systems approach, according to Jordan (1997), is "present situation analysis," an ongoing assessment of a large number of variables, including the learner, teacher, institution, curriculum, assessment, and the interaction among them. Jordan believes that subsequent needs analyses have been "refinements to the starting positions of present situation and future/target situation" (p. 25).

Target Situation Analyses. During the early to mid-1980s, EAP researchers in U.S. universities conducted target situation analyses to discover the skills and assignments ESL students were likely to encounter in future academic classes across the curriculum (Horowitz, 1986b; Johns, 1981; Ostler, 1980). These studies were, in part, a reaction against the growing interest in process approaches in L1 and L2 composition research and teaching. EAP specialists were concerned that the focus on students' writing processes detracted from what they saw as the business at hand: preparing students for courses across the curriculum. They rejected the premise of process advocates, such as Zamel (1976, 1982), who argued that if students were guided through the same types of activities carried out by professional writers—invention, drafting, revising and editing—they could apply these practices to any assignment they met. Horowitz (1986a) was especially critical of the emphasis on conferencing and revision, pointing out that some types of academic writing, such as essay examinations, do not call for multiple drafts. Instead, they are timed writings designed to test knowledge: product, not process. Horowitz (1986a), therefore, believed that process writing was inadequate, perhaps harmful, preparation for the demands of academic courses.

To discover those demands and provide "realistic advice about appropriate discourse structures for specific tasks" in EAP (p. 447), Horowitz (1986b) surveyed writing-assignment handouts and essay-examination questions from 36 faculty (out of 750 contacted) at a midwestern university. According to Horowitz, the most important finding of his survey was that the writing tasks were highly controlled by faculty who offered detailed instructions about content and organization. His data analysis includes a taxonomy of writing tasks, including summaries of/reactions to a reading; annotated bibliographies; syntheses of multiple sources; and research projects. It also includes a set of skills required for carrying out those tasks: selecting relevant data from sources; reorganizing data in response to a question; encoding data into academic English. In his pedagogical recommendations, Horowitz proposes exercises to "simulate university writing tasks in a practical way" (p. 455) and to offer students ways to work on "information-processing problems" (p. 460).

Having concluded from his survey that "[g]enerally speaking, the academic writer's task is not to create personal meaning, but to find, organize, and present data according to fairly explicit instructions," Horowitz (1986b) recommends an emphasis in EAP on "recognition and reorganization of data" rather than "invention and personal discovery," tenets of process writing. (p. 455) Perhaps revealing a lack of conviction about the generalizability of his findings, Horowitz tentatively proposes EAP curricula based on his small sample at a single university. Yet, he also calls on EAP teachers to conduct their own target situation analyses. That is, he simultaneously recommends restructuring of ESL teaching based on an admittedly limited survey and suggests further research in local contexts to bring EAP instruction in line with the cognitive and linguistic demands of college courses in those institutions.

A similar tension appears in Johns' (1981) report of a survey of 140 faculty at San Diego State University. The author makes recommendations based on her small sample and calls for further research at her own institution and at others to "teach more of the skills that the students will actually need" (p. 56). In her study, Johns asked respondents to rank English skills in order of importance for a particular class they taught. Finding that reading and listening were ranked highest among faculty teaching lower- and upper-division classes, Johns (1981) recommends "systematic teaching of listening and note-taking" (p. 56) in EAP classes and a de-emphasis on speaking and writing, except in the service of lecture and textbook comprehension: "Writing, for example, could involve the paraphrase or summary of reading materials or the organization and rewriting of lecture notes" (p. 56). Curiously, the finding that the majority of faculty, except those in engineering, ranked general English above specific-purposes English is dismissed as a matter of ignorance: "There could be a number of reasons for the General English preferences, the most compelling of which is that most faculty do not understand the nature and breadth of ESP. They tend to think of it as an aspect of the discipline that has to do with vocabulary alone"(p. 54).

Although Horowitz and Johns seem to recognize the limitations of their research, they are nonetheless prepared to generalize their findings to other EAP settings. Materials writers also subscribed to the idea that skills taught in an EAP class would transfer to students' future academic classes. Textbooks based on this assumption proliferated during the 1980s and 1990s, some of which dealt with English for general academic purposes (EGAP) while others, classified as English for specific academic purposes (ESAP), focused on a single field, such as economics, engineering, and business.

Despite the appearance of numerous skills-based EGAP and ESAP textbooks, doubts about the generalizability of study skills from one context to another began to emerge, leading to an increase in more contextualized EAP research and instruction as the following sections show.

Present Situation Analyses. Needs analysis based solely on surveys and questionnaires were supplanted in the late 1980s with present situation analysis taking a greater number of variables into account, following the Council of Europe's comprehensive, ongoing needs analyses (Johns, 1990a; Prior, 1991,1995; Ramani, Chacko, Singh, & Glendinning, 1988). This research aims to reveal not only the types of texts assigned but also reactions of students to assignments and the processes they go through in fulfilling them as well as faculty reactions to student participation and writing. Teaching as an interactive social practice is recognized in this research, which includes in-depth interviews and observation of faculty and students and, in some cases, ongoing revision of EAP instruction based on feedback and evaluation.

One example of present situation analysis is the ethnographic approach to EAP syllabus design of Ramani et al. (1988) at the Indian Institute of Science in Bangalore. Dissatisfied with register and discourse analysis as tools to guide English language instruction, these colleagues from the Foreign Language Section conducted ethnographic research over 1 month in four departments. Their data collection consisted of seven steps:

1. specify the learners;
2. analyze their needs;
3. specify enabling objections;
4. select or evolve materials;
5. identify appropriate teaching/learning activities;
6. evaluate;
7. revise.

Step 2 is further broken down into more detailed data collection taking students' and teachers' views into account:

1. observe students in their natural academic environment ("what the normal day of a student in a particular department is like" (p. 84);
2. ask the students about their communication practices, needs, and problems;
3. ask the subject specialists;
4. ask the language specialists.

Ramani et al. (1988) found their colleagues in other departments receptive to interviews and clear about a range of issues from the larger goals of their field and department to the communicative practices required by their courses.

During unstructured interviews, the teacher/researchers learned about distinctions between professional genres they had been previously unaware of and about the recent stress on critical reading and discussion of journal articles in management courses. These and other findings led to changes in English language courses, including an increase in problem-solving activities carried out in pair and group work. The researchers do not claim that their findings are applicable to other settings. Rather, they recommend ethnographic approaches as a way to collaborate with other faculty "to articulate and understand the complexity and specificity of the communication" (Ramani et al., 1988, p. 88) in the institutions in which they teach.

Prior's (1991, 1995) research is also ethnographic. Influenced by "situated" L1 composition research, his three studies of a graduate seminar in second-language education aimed for "a fuller examination of the literate processes involved in academic work" than is offered through analysis of assignment guidelines or student texts alone (Prior, 1995, p. 49). The data included observations of seminar meetings, interviews with students and the professor about assignments and course goals, and "text-based interviews" (Prior, 1991, p. 273), with the professor sharing his reactions to particular student papers. Prior chronicles the history of selected assignments, from preliminary in-class explanations by the professor to clarification, negotiation and enactment of the guidelines by the students in dialogue with the professor. He describes making and carrying out writing assignments in the graduate seminar as a complicated and interactive "indeterminate" process characterized by "order, convention, and continuity," on the one hand, and "chance, anomaly, and rupture," on the other (Prior, 1991, p. 304). For example, to his surprise, Prior discovered that students relied more on their prior experience in school, on the assigned readings, and on their perceptions of the professors' interests and biases in carrying out assignments than on the professor's initial guidelines. He also notes that some of the international students in the seminar were able to prevail on the professor to reduce the number of reading assignments and drop one of the writing assignments, revealing a degree of flexibility that would not have appeared if the data had only included the original syllabus and assignment guidelines.

Prior's (1995) view is that surveys and questionnaires offer EAP useful information about the linguistic and rhetorical structure of academic texts, but that they are limited due to their neglect of "situated processes and resources students use in producing writing and professors use in responding to it" (p. 77). He cautions readers not to transform his findings into "abstract, anonymous structures occurring anytime, anywhere" (p. 55) but rather to conceptualize academic writing tasks as speech genres "unfold[ing] in concrete situations at specific times with particular participants" (p. 77). These studies will complicate the job of teachers, materials writers, test makers and researchers, according to Prior, but the benefit is that they will honor the complexity and dialogic nature of academic teaching and learning.

Like Prior, Johns (1988a, 1990a), in a retreat from her earlier research (Johns, 1981), questions the generalizability of precourse needs analysis from the context in which it was carried out to others. Reviewing L1 studies on writing-across-the-curriculum, she notes that university courses are idiosyncratic, even those within the same department. Individual professors' idiosyncrasies, she concludes, make it difficult for needs analysis to predict the demands students will face in academic courses. Therefore, according to Johns, target situation analysis is an inadequate tool for EAP curriculum development. In its place, she recommends ethnographic needs analysis in linked EAP/content courses, thereby combining research and teaching. That is, as far as Johns is concerned, EAP research is best carried out by students and teachers in a collaborative, cross-curricular effort. Her description of linked courses at San Diego State University demonstrates how student research informed EAP teaching (Johns, 1990a).

Non-native students enrolled in the linked courses were asked to keep journals. Included in the journals were documentation of roles the students and their professor of Western Civilization were supposed to play in that course; the topics dealt with in the syllabus; the relationship of the topics to each other; and the various activities and conventions carried out in the content class. As the semester progressed, students reflected on their participation in that class, including their difficulties with reading and writing, offering the EAP teacher information and guidance about how to proceed and what to emphasize. Johns (1990a) concludes from her analysis of the students' journals, and the discussions and intervention they triggered, that the ideal setting for EAP is linked courses where language instruction is contextualized: "If there is any way for direct contact with and discussion about content classes to take place, as it does in the program mentioned here, then more ideal teaching and learning circumstances can result" (p. 225).

Benson (1989) conducted an ethnographic study of a Saudi Arabian master's candidate in public administration at a U.S. university, examining the experience of an Arabic-speaking student navigating the complexities of academic study in English. In particular, Benson wanted to document the role listening played in his subject's learning, participation, and performance in one course. His data included taped lectures; lecture notes of his subject, some of his fellow students, and those of the professor; as well as interviews with his subject and the professor. Benson triangulates his data, showing what was said in class, what was written in lecture notes, and what his subject said retrospectively, after attending lectures. His analysis shows, among other things, that his subject recorded what he viewed to be main points but ignored other rhetorical moves, such as teacher/student interaction and teacher asides, which the professor believed offered equally important information. In addition, Benson (1989) notes that "in a highly verbal and participatory class, Hamad [his subject] never said a word. He was one of only two who remained silent throughout the 15 weeks" (p. 439). In drawing implications for EAP instruction from his study, Benson is critical of typical listening activities stressing comprehension as a one-way process of information absorption by students rather than as an interactive process involving both teaching and learning. He recommends EAP courses at U.S. universities that could engender the types of interactions he found in the lectures he studied where the students were expected not just to record facts but also to be aware of "attitudinal and affective factors that modify course content in various ways" (p. 441). That is, like Johns, he believes that students need to understand academic course work as more than information processing. Instead, each course presents cultural and intellectual challenges that may differ from ones students are accustomed to.

One way to contextualize EAP instruction is through linked courses, Johns' preferred mode of instruction, where students enroll concurrently in language and content courses, in which the materials and methods of both may be related. These courses require a certain amount of coordination not available in all institutions. Yet, they have been popular on campuses aiming to mainstream students into an academic curriculum. Due to the predominance of linked courses in U.S. undergraduate institutions, I present them here in a separate section rather than including them with the section on study skills, as is done in most overviews of EAP. In addition, the focus of the examples of linked courses, in the following section, is less on skills and more on collaboration across the curriculum.

Linked Courses

Although ESL faculty have experimented with linked courses since the late 1970s, this approach to EAP gained wider acceptance during the mid-1980s and continues into the present. With research evidence pointing to professors' varying expectations not only in different disciplines but "even different classes within a discipline" (Prior, 1991, p. 270), the need for well-contextualized EAP instruction based on continuous feedback from students and faculty was increasingly clear. Also, with little research evidence of transfer of skills from one context (the EAP classroom) to another (the content course), some EAP specialists have sought ways to join these contexts by forming partnerships with colleagues in other departments. They offer linked, adjunct, and team-taught courses, matching language instruction to the assignments, activities, and discourse of the content courses with which they are paired. The goal is to give students "immediate assistance with their difficulties as they arise," support not available when the "subject teacher or the language teacher [is] working in isolation" (Johns & Dudley-Evans, 1980, p. 8). According to Swales (1988), team-teaching represents "the ESP practitioner's growing concern with the total educational environment of the student" (p. 137).

One influence on paired courses in EAP is the language-across-the-curriculum (LAC) movement in the United Kingdom, exported to U.S. universities as writing-across-the-curriculum (WAC) in the 1980s. As early as 1966, members of the London Association of Teachers of English met to discuss the relationship between language and learning and to urge schools to work out a language policy for subjects across the curriculum. According to Britton (1982), one aim was to encourage children to use expressive talk and writing when learning new material, that is, "language in which we 'first-draft' our tentative or speculative ideas" (p. 181). Children's informal ways of speaking were seen as a way to explore new material and work toward understanding complex content. U.S. educators, such as Fulwiler and Young (1990), embraced the idea of expressive writing across the curriculum and conducted workshops at the University of Vermont and other universities to encourage the use of journals in all subjects areas, not just English.

Hirsch's (1988) tutoring program at Hostos Community College, the City University of New York's bilingual (Spanish/English) college, is a good example of the use of expressive talk and writing in EAP. Concerned that students who, despite having exited from the college's ESL program, have difficulty reading textbooks, understanding lectures, and passing tests in their academic classes, Hirsch developed small tutor-led groups, of between three and eight students, linked to General Biology, Introduction to Business, and Early Childhood Education. The tutors, graduate and undergraduate students from public and private colleges, underwent 36 hours of preservice training as "facilitators of student learning" (p. 74) and ongoing training during the semesters they tutored. They were required to attend the content classes for which they were tutors and to meet periodically with the content teachers. Tutoring sessions offered opportunities for "expressive, exploratory talk and writing," including "students paraphrasing concepts, using learning logs, writing tutor- or pupil-generated assignments, reading from their papers, or holding frequent group discussions" (p. 73). Hirsch found that students who participated in the tutoring groups received a higher final mean grade than those in the control group and twice as many As. In addition, the classroom attendance rate was higher among participants than nonparticipants. Hirsch (1988) attributes the program's effectiveness to the "importance of expressive language, and especially talk, as a contributor to ESL student learning" (p. 82).

Like Hirsch, Blakely (1995) was troubled that students who had successfully completed ESL courses offered at the University of Rhode Island struggled with their mainstream academic course work. He therefore developed a program allowing non-native students (NNS) to continue studying English while pursuing their undergraduate degrees; the language instruction would be directly connected to the content courses they took. In an interesting variation on Hirsch's tutoring model, Blakely recruited undergraduates who were enrolled as students in the class for which they would be tutors. That is, he paired "high-achieving native speakers with at-risk linguistic minority speakers" (p. 4) within the same course. Each semester, 15 native-speaking students, called *fellows*, participated in a 15-week training seminar for which they received three credits. The first part of the training, "Who," dealt with immigrants in the United States, the population comprising the NNS students at the University of Rhode Island. The second part, "What," covered second-language acquisition theory and practice. The third part, "How," dealt with what to do in meetings with NNS students. Blakely stresses the distinction between tutoring and the collaborative studying the program encouraged. The fellows were not peer tutors, a designation implying a power differential between giver and receiver. Rather, they saw themselves as "'privileged collaborators in learning,' the privilege being their native understanding of the language of instruction" (p. 5). Indeed, aside from the cognitive and linguistic benefits of study groups, there were social gains as well. Not only were averages for fellows and their NNS classmates significantly higher than those of nonparticipants, but those who participated in the groups reported a new appreciation for students with whom they had previously had no contact. That is, the program raised the profile of NNS students who had been marginalized and ignored on this campus and in the courses where they were performing very poorly. The social connections Blakely's program encouraged seem to have increased the retention of NNS students.

One more feature of the University of Rhode Island program is worth noting: interaction between the fellows and content faculty. Blakely reports that fellows were required to meet periodically with their professors to discuss the study sessions and let them know about any difficulties they and the NNS students might have been having. As a result of these meetings, content faculty made modifications, such as meeting with NNS students and fellows before exams, allowing extra time for writing assignments, simplifying language, and using more visuals during lectures. Although these changes are not a main goal of the English Language Fellows Program, they point to an area that is sometimes overlooked in EAP: The role of the content teacher in facilitating learning.

Instructional modifications by content faculty are highlighted in Haas, Smoke, and Hernandez (1991), whose account of their "collaborative model" of paired courses is a transcript of their retrospective conversation about the developmental and ESL writing courses taught by Haas and Smoke at Hunter College, CUNY, paired with Hernandez's social sciences lecture course, "Conquered Peoples in America." In addition to meeting before the semester began to plan ways to coordinate instruction, the three met weekly to discuss assignments, students, and supplementary material. Hernandez highlights several modifications he made as a result of feedback from Haas and Smoke. For example, learning that his lectures were based on the incorrect assumption that the students had a background in geography and the origins of human beings, he decided to include maps and anthropological information in future lectures. In addition, he changed his view of writing—from a means of testing knowledge to a means of learning:

> During our collaboration, I began to ask students to write informally and I responded in writing, so they understood if their comments were effective or missed the point. At first, some students only turned in a sentence or two, thinking that was enough but when they realized that I preferred exploration to a quick answer, their next compositions changed radically. Students were much more expansive when they knew I was commenting on their ideas. (Haas, Smoke, & Hernandez, 1991, pp. 122–123)

Smoke and Haas also discuss ways they modified their teaching in response to Hernandez's course. For example, Haas abandoned planned lessons when students came into her class, fresh from a lecture, wanting to continue discussing the ideas. She found herself listening more than speaking, learning more than teaching on those occasions. Like Blakely, authors Haas, Smoke, and Hernandez (1991) note that the collaboration between teachers and among the students created a community resulting in higher grades for the participants than for nonparticipants in their program.

The previous two examples of linked courses bring up the issue of collaboration between language and content teachers as a central feature of linked courses. Barron (1992) offers a schema to categorize what he calls "cooperative relationships between ESP units and other departments" (p. 1) to take various levels of involvement into account. At the low end of the involvement continuum is the subject-specialist informant, who offers information to the ESP teacher about the "content and organisation of texts and on the processes of their subject" (p. 2). This information is used by the ESP teacher to inform materials development and lessons related to the subject; there is no formal link between ESL and content classes. At the high end of the continuum are team-taught courses where the faculty cooperate to the fullest extent, working out a joint syllabus, materials, methodology, and assessment. Barron describes his own experience as "collaborative teaching" (p. 4), a relationship he considers to involve a lower degree of cooperation than team teaching, in part because there are two separate classrooms rather than a shared one. At Papua New Guinea University of Technology, he taught language and communication skills classes to first-year architecture students concurrently enrolled in a 7-hour studio class where they learned drawing and other architectural skills. Barron and the architecture teacher developed a series of joint projects intended to call on the language and architecture skills that were evaluated by both teachers.

To finish this history of EAP, I now turn to the most recent development, genre analysis. Although Dudley-Evans and St. John (1998) find this to be "an extremely useful tool of analysis" rather than "a new movement in the field" (p. 31), genre analysis has nonetheless captured the interest of various ESP/EAP researchers, cited next.

Genre Analysis

Genre analysis reflects ESP/EAP's traditional attention to linguistic features of texts, their rhetorical purposes, and pedagogical application. Yet, genres are not simply texts to be analyzed for their grammatical and discoursal features. Rather, genre is "a social activity of a typical and recognizable kind in a community, which is realised in language" (Mauranen, 1993). That is, genres go beyond text to take social purposes into account, including ways members of discourse communities are guided by shared rhetorical purposes when they speak and write. They are "typified responses to events that recur over time and space" (Berkenkotter & Huckin, 1995, p.151). For example, members of the English-language teaching community follow certain conventions when giving conference talks or writing articles, making these genres recognizable to their listeners and readers. Participating in these social acts solidifies one's membership in the community.

Bhatia (1993) contrasts genre analysis with register and rhetorical analysis, earlier types of EAP research discussed before, placing them all under the discourse-analysis rubric and then making distinctions. He categorizes register analysis and grammatical–rhetorical analysis as *discourse analysis as description*, which "typically concentrates on the linguistic aspects of text construction and interpretation" (p. 2) and therefore offers "insufficient explanation of sociocultural institutions and organizational constraints" (p. 10) shaping discourse. Genre analysis, categorized by

Bhatia as *discourse analysis as explanation,* on the other hand, "goes beyond such a description to rationalize conventional aspects of genre construction and interpretation" (p. 2). It is concerned with answering the question:"Why are specific discourse-genres written and used by the specialist communities the way they are?" (p. 11). It aims to explain "why a particular type of conventional codification of meaning is considered appropriate to a particular institutionalized sociocultural setting" (p. 5).

These questions interest both EAP specialists and L1 rhetoricians (sometimes called *new rhetoric researchers*) such as Bazerman and Myers. They have carried out situated studies on, for example, the research processes of scientists and social scientists (Bazerman, 1988) and how two biologists worked to get their research funded and published (Myers, 1990). However, although L1 rhetoricians share an interest with EAP researchers in genre, their concerns and approaches to genre analysis differ. Hyon (1996) characterizes those differences, as well as ways Australian genre research differs from the other two.

According to Hyon, EAP genre research has concentrated mainly on the "formal characteristics of genres while focusing less on the specialized functions of texts and their surrounding social contexts" (p. 695). So, although rationales for genre research in EAP such as Bhatia's, mention social context, the studies are more concerned with textual features, such as discourse moves, than with particular situations and communities. New rhetoric studies, such as those of Bazerman, Prior, and Myers, on the other hand, are concerned with the role genres play, their "social purposes" or "actions" (Hyon, 1996) in particular settings. The new rhetoricians carry out ethnographic research "rather than linguistic methods for analyzing texts, offering thick descriptions of academic and professional contexts surrounding genres and the actions texts perform within these situations" (Hyon, 1996, p. 696). Like EAP genre studies, Australian genre research is linguistic, focused on textual structures, yet the types of genres studied are not academic and professional; rather, they are school- and workplace-based, reflecting a different set of goals, as shown next.

Hyon (1996) attributes the differences in the three genre traditions to varying contexts and goals. EAP, influenced by linguistics and applied linguistics, is mainly interested in applying its research findings to helping NNS students "master the functions and linguistic conventions of texts" (p. 698). That is, the primary goal is to help students fulfill the requirements of academic and professional settings so that they can "succeed" (p. 700). (In chap. 3, I discuss this goal as an ideological stance; for now, I accept Hyon's terms). The Australians, who analyze primary and secondary school genres, are also interested in helping students "succeed" though they claim that the "powerful" genres they study and teach will "empower" (p. 701) previously underserved children, including immigrants. New rhetoric researchers, by contrast, are less sanguine about the applicability of their studies to teaching.

Bazerman (1998) characterizes the difference between his research and that of Swales (1990) as a contrast between two traditions: rhetoric and linguistics. The rhetorical tradition, from which Bazerman comes, uses literary techniques, in an "ad hoc descriptive tradition . . . noticing a variety of things that might be going on in the text but not through any particular linguistic method" (p. 106). Swales' training in linguistics, on the other hand, led him to focus on moves analysis and linguistic features, such as tense and modality. Although Bazerman values Swales' and other linguists' research for offering rigorous, precise analysis "with which you could try to tie things down" (p. 108), he also cautions against dealing with genre "in too codified a way" (p. 109). Yet, he finds Swales' (1990) "create a research space" (CARS) model, discussed next, to be useful in teaching graduate students in the social sciences, though less useful with literature students.

In his analyses of research article introductions, Swales (1990) aimed to discover how scientists establish the context and credibility for their own research, in light of previous studies, in the introductions they write to research articles. Yet, Swales did not simply discuss his findings about the rhetorical moves in scientific research article introductions. He translated them into a model, the "create a research space" (CARS) model, that could be used to teach this part of the research article as a genre (Swales, 1990, p. 140). This model has been adopted in various teaching situations, with mixed results: Master's of Science students in a British university (Dudley-Evans, 1995); undergraduate science students in a U.S. university (Jacoby, Leech, & Holten, 1995); and undergraduate first-year general education students at a U.S. university (Johns, 1995).

Dudley-Evans (1995) applies a modification of the CARS model to teaching academic writing to international graduate students in 1-year master's of science and PhD programs at the University of Birmingham. Students are offered a common-core class in which they develop rhetorical awareness by answering a series of questions about the patterns of organization of a text and why those particular patterns are "favored by those in the discourse community" (Dudley-Evans, 1995, p. 296). The students then apply move analysis to sections of research articles and theses, including the introduction, method, and discussion sections. The first exercise carried out to develop awareness of moves is for students to reorder the scrambled sentences of a research article introduction and then to discuss the correct order. They are then introduced to the revised four-move CARS model (establish the field; summarize the previous research; prepare for present research; introduce present research) and encouraged to practice "the language used to express each of the four moves" (Dudley-Evans, 1995, p. 300). Finally students are asked to write a "simulation of either a full report or a full section of an article or thesis based on some data or information provided" (Dudley-Evans, 1995, p. 301). According to Dudley-Evans (1995), these activities contribute to students' ability to apply "general knowledge of genre conventions and other aspects of writing they have gained from the general classes to actual assignments or examination answers" (p. 304), although no follow-up studies of student performance in subject-specific classes are cited.

Jacoby, Leech, and Holten (1995) describe a developmental writing course for non-native undergraduate science majors at UCLA. The goals of the course are to introduce "formal aspects of scientific writing" (p. 353) as well as to promote writing proficiency among these inexperienced writers. The authors see their charge as an "uneasy partnership" between product ("textual conventions of the scientific research report") and process ("strategies for revising, . . . shaping texts, . . . and responding effectively to their own and others' writing"; Jacoby, Leech, & Holten, 1995, p. 353). The example they offer of this partnership is an instructional unit on teaching the discourse structure and lexical and grammatical features of the discussion section of a research report. When beginning this unit, students have already written a draft of the introduction to a study they have not read, although they have read previous studies on which this one is based. After receiving feedback on their draft, students are given a table or graph showing the results of the current study. They are then taken through a series of activities, including a handout matching lexical choices with discourse moves from "authentic" discussion sections, helping them write their own sections. The teachers also involve the students in self-reflection exercises to assess their understanding of the discourse conventions and their writing processes. The authors claim success for their course: "Rather than ignore or reduce this [rhetorical, textual, linguistic, and cognitive] complexity, our approach has been to find systematic ways of engaging students in discovering the richness of scientific argument so that they can successfully produce their own first attempts at experimental report writing" (Jacoby et al., 1995, p. 367). How that success is measured, however, is not discussed.

The students in Jacoby, Leech, and Holten's program are undergraduate science majors. Johns' (1995) students are first-semester general education students whose low scores on the writing entrance exam have placed them in an ESL adjunct program; they are considered "at-risk" (p. 281). Johns discusses the curriculum of an ESL writing class, a combination of study skills and genre teaching, linked to a general education geography class. The geography course was a large lecture class in which students listened, took notes, read textbook chapters, and were given examinations, mainly multiple-choice. She also mentions that the geography professor did not attempt to "initiate students into the discipline; nothing was provided that would increase their awareness of authentic genres" (p. 283). Despite, or perhaps because of, the geography professor's lack of attention to "authentic genres," the adjunct writing course curriculum revolved around a data-driven paper based on interviews, a library assignment, and a journal article abstract. In addition, the geography teacher assigned an out-of-class essay and an in-class examination response.

Johns (1995) describes two assignments from the writing course in detail: the data-driven paper and the abstract. She calls the first a "classroom genre" and the second an "authentic genre" (p. 282). A classroom genre (CG), according to Johns, is a type of assignment traditionally required of undergraduate students, such as essay exams, summaries, lecture notes, and research papers. Faculty assign classroom genres, Johns claims, out of habit, because they are "reminiscent of their own undergraduate experience rather than of the discipline they have chosen" (p. 282). Authentic genres (AG), on the other hand, are those "employed to communicate among experts in a discipline (e.g., "the bid, the proposal, the memo, the report, or the journal article"; Johns, 1995, p. 282). The responsibility of the adjunct class, according to Johns, is to teach both CGs (helping students fulfill current assignments), and AGs, so that students can "move beyond the requirements of the CGs to initiation into an academic or professional discourse community" (p. 283).

The AG assignment Johns discusses included reading a published research article on methods used in the conservation of Polynesian birds, suggested to the EAP professor by the geography professor, and writing an abstract based on this article. The series of activities related to this assignment began with studying the title and list of references at the end of the article, then writing an invented bibliographic entry using the style found in the list, and discussing different types of referencing. Johns next asked students to analyze the article's introduction using Swales' CARS model, followed by a discussion of the article's headings, maps, and citations. Finally, the students wrote an abstract (the original one had been removed), based on the headings. According to Johns, the abstract assignment was "a very difficult one" for the students. She adds that "[m]ost did not get to the core of the article" (p. 288). Nor did the students have much success with the next part of the assignment—writing a formal letter to the Tonga Parliament, as if they were the authors of the research article, "discussing their findings and suggesting measures for conservation of wildlife" (p. 288). Johns admits that students "had difficulty" with this letter-writing assignment, "a formidable task" (p. 288).

Johns' (1995) students' difficulties with genre-based assignments raise questions about applying genre-research findings to teaching situations other than ones in which the research was carried out, a concern raised by Prior (1998). His case studies of graduate seminars in language education, geography, American studies, and sociology challenge the notion of genres as predictable and stable text types across and within disciplines. Rather, Prior's (1998) research reveals that "specific writing tasks are rarely routine, involving complexly situated and novel features" (p. 64). Due to the situated nature of writing tasks, Prior recommends further research into ways students and teachers coconstruct assignments under the specific conditions of a particular class. He also cautions teachers not to assume a congruence between "what students need for success in classes," "what they need for institutional progress," and "their needs in professional work after they graduate" (Prior, 1995, p. 76), pointing out that these may vary. Given the limited transfer between "well-structured lessons," for example those developed by EAP teachers, and "complex settings" students will encounter in their academic content classes, Prior proposes engaging students in "dynamic, situated, interaction" in such settings as linked classes and using tools such as dialogue journals, to facilitate "communicative flexibility" (p. 77). This formulation, he believes, may hold greater promise for EAP than attempts to apply genre- research findings from one context to another. This is not to say that genre analysis has no place in EAP, but, rather, that the situated nature of teaching and learning requires context-sensitive curricula based on classroom research, called for by McDonough (1986), cited earlier in this chapter. According to Prior (1995), "[i]f academic discourse and academic environments are complex, constructed and unfolding events and not closed systems susceptible to taxonomic and rule-oriented description, then we cannot simply specify and teach 'academic writing tasks'" (pp. 76–77), that is, a reified notion of genre.

SUMMARY

The strength of EAP has been its sensitivity to context. Yet, this overview of its 30-year history shows that the definition of context has been revised continually. During the years of register and rhetorical analysis, vocabulary and grammatical choices were the context, the focus of research and teaching. Later, as attention shifted to communication and learning, skills and learning strategies became the areas of attention. More recently, with acknowledgment of the social construction of knowledge and language as discourse, social practices have become central to EAP research and teaching. This does not mean that EAP no longer attends to texts or learning processes. In fact, Candlin (1999) believes that EAP has arrived at a reconciliation of "texts, processes, and practices" with its focus on the "interconnection of the three in particular discourse communities." That is, form, cognitive processes, and institutional practices are integrated in the current interest in "dynamic interdiscursivity." How that integration will manifest itself in research and teaching is an ongoing question. It remains to be seen whether McDonough's (1986) "classroom-initiated research" informed by theory will prevail.

Despite EAP's attention to context, however, one central assumption guiding EAP research and teaching has not been adequately addressed in its official history: That its purpose is to prepare students unquestioningly for institutional and faculty expectations (Benesch, 1993). This is one of the themes taken up in chapter 3, a study of the literature offering critiques of EAP from outside the field. First, however, in chapter 2, I discuss the unofficial history of ESP/EAP that is, their political and economic roots.

Political and Economic
Roots of EAP

The previous chapter presents a chronology of EAP's goals, research, and instructional practices over the last 30 years, from inside the field. This chapter is a view from the outside, an unofficial history, including political and economic issues not traditionally taken up in the literature. It examines how English became the dominant language of science, technology, and business and why, from an ideological point of view, ESP/EAP responded as they did. Included in this chapter is a discussion of a 1971 document revealing the willingness of ESP/EAP specialists to accept target requirements unconditionally and uncritically as the basis of instruction. Also included is Phillipson's (1992) study of the economic roots of English language teaching during the post-World War II period.

POLITICAL AND ECONOMIC ROOTS OF ESP/EAP

The discussion begins with two quotes, one from a frequently cited early English-for-science-and-technology document (Barber, 1962), the other from a 1971 conference paper I have never seen cited in the ESP literature, although it has been preserved as an ERIC document (130 525):

> During recent years, English has increasingly become a medium for the teaching and learning of other subjects. This use of English as an auxiliary language is especially important in those countries where a great deal of university-teaching is carried out in English (e.g., India); but it is also important in many other countries, which rely to a great extent on textbooks written in English, especially at the university level. This dependence on textbooks in English seems to be particularly marked in scientific and technical subjects, and there must be many thousands of students of these subjects who rely wholly or largely on books published in Britain and the United States. It is

therefore of interest to teachers of English abroad, and especially of course to those who teach English to scientists and technologists, to examine the characteristics of scientific English . . . (Barber, 1962, cited in Swales, 1988)

As long as ARAMCO [Arabian American Oil Company] has been involved in formal training—and this (in one form or another) covers thirty years—there has been a special emphasis on English language training. *English is the language of oil technology and of the people who work in oil* [emphasis mine] . . . I think we must say that the principal reason for English training is to enable the Saudi to get the technical training that is required by the oil industry and to be able to read the job manuals and other printed materials relevant to oil production. (Johnson, 1971, pp. 63–64, cited in proceedings of Conference on Adult English for National Development, ERIC Document 130 525)

⌈The previous two quotes illustrate, respectively, what has been emphasized in the ESP literature and what has been left out. The first, from a sanctioned text, is an example of ESP's discourse of neutrality and consensus, shown in its unquestioned acceptance of the dominance of English in overseas universities, textbooks, and science and technology, presenting that dominance as naturally occurring and inevitable. I review this quote for what it demonstrates about ESP's official history. The second quote is from a document I analyze for what it reveals about efforts of governments and private companies to promote English worldwide, for political and commercial purposes, and the relationship of those efforts to ESP.⌋

Examining the First Quote: ESP's Official History

Barber's (1962) rationale for studying and teaching scientific English exemplifies how ESP specialists have traditionally presented their work. According to this version of events, EST was the logical response to the inevitable rise of English as the dominant language of science and technology. The increased influence of English is presented as a natural occurrence. For example, Dudley-Evans and St. John (1998) describe the "flowering" of ESP resulting from "general developments in the world economy in the 1950s and 1960s," including the "increased use of English as the international language of science, technology, and business" (p. 19). In their 30-year retrospective of ESP, Johns and Dudley-Evans (1991) discuss the "ascendancy" of English in "international science, technology, and trade" and the increase in demand for English for specific purposes around the world as a result of that "ascendancy" (p. 297). Flowerdew (1990) describes interest in ESP as a function of "market forces," creating a "continuing demand" for these courses in developing countries, in the United States and in the United Kingdom, with ESP and business English "spreading to hitherto relatively untapped areas" (p. 326). Left unexamined is the role of governments, foundations, and private companies in the "ascendency" of English, that is, their role in creating and cultivating markets, driving the demand for English-speaking workers and customers in those countries where markets were established by U.S. and U.K. companies.

In their overview of ESP's history, Hutchinson and Waters (1987) touch on its economic roots in the Middle East, referring to "a massive flow of funds and Western expertise into the oil-rich countries" following the "Oil Crises of the early 1970s" (p. 7). However, they offer no analysis of the impact of Western funds and advisors, accepting ESP uncritically as a function of "deliver[ing] the required goods" (p. 7). In addition, they portray ESP students in those countries as wholehearted endorsers of this well-funded enterprise: ". . . as English became the accepted international language of technology and commerce, it created a new generation of learners who knew specifically why they were learning a language" (p. 6). Possible tensions between native and imported languages and cultures are not considered.

Swales (1977) also discusses the "increase" (p. 36) in English language teaching and ESP in the Middle East in the early 1970s. He sets out to explore how the "need to use English as a medium of instruction" in countries such as Libya, Iran, Turkey, and Sudan "has arisen" (p.36), but the analysis is tautological. Swales attributes the "growth of English" to "the incredibly rapid quantitative expansion of education facilities in the tertiary sector, particularly in the so-called 'petro-dollar' states" and the concomitant need for teachers "from outside the area" (p. 36) due to a lack of local specialists. Swales notes that teachers were recruited by UNESCO, the British Council, and other agencies, although their motivation for promoting ESP in these countries is not explained.

Instead, Swales offers the following reasons for why the majority of the newly formed postsecondary institutions in the Middle East were established as anglophone: "the impossibility of having all the staff speakers of the local language, a predominately technological bias in the institutions, the thought behind many of the aid agreements, the fact that English is studied for several years at school, and links, both old and new, with Britain and America" (p. 36). Left unexplored is the colonial legacy of English language teaching in the region's primary and secondary schools, the mysterious "thought behind many of the aid agreements," and the types of links being forged between British and U.S. governments and companies at that time concerning these new anglophone institutions in the oil-rich countries. Also unexplored is why a technological bias necessarily led educational institutions to adopt English as the medium of instruction. By failing to explain these factors, Swales' version endorses ESP as a necessary response to an inevitable sequence of events.

An underlying assumption of Swales' (1977) discussion of ESP in the Middle East at that time is that it was an unquestioningly good service for all involved. Possible conflicts are not acknowledged, as if the interests of, for example, the British Council and undergraduate students in these countries were perfectly aligned, with everyone benefitting equally. This assumption is part of what I call an "ideology of pragmatism" (Benesch, 1993), getting the job done with no critical analysis of the consequences for the various parties, some of which may have much to gain at the expense of others. Rather than concerning himself with political and economic questions, Swales (1977) outlines conditions favoring ESP in the Middle East, as well as obstacles to those courses. The principle positive condition he lists is "outside support," including the British Council's "energetic promotional role" (p. 36) and the Ford Foundation's sponsorship of ESP specialists. Among the obstacles he lists are a high turnover among ESP teachers, leading to a lack of staffing continuity.

Missing from all of these discussions of ESP's origins are the coordinated efforts of U.K. and U.S. governmental agencies, private foundations, universities, and private industry to vigorously promote English language teaching at home and abroad and to support English for specific purposes to further certain political and economic interests. In the case of Swales (1977), even when he mentions these agencies, he leaves out the reasons for their presence in various countries. The quietism in the ESP/EAP community about the colonial history of Middle Eastern countries and the desire of the United States and United Kingdom to maintain control of their oil is remarkable. Yet, without an analysis of the underlying motivation and goals, it is impossible for ESP teachers to come to terms with the ethics of their practice, to ask who they are working for, and to examine possible consequences of their teaching. In the final chapter of this book, I propose the formation of an ethics of EAP as a way to work toward more reflexive and critical practice. To delve into the ethics of ESP in the period referred to by Hutchinson and Waters (1987) and Swales (1977), the early 1970s in the Middle East, I now turn to the second quote.

Examining the Second Quote:
ESP's Unofficial History

The second quote from a paper given at the 1971 Adult English for National Development Conference (". . . .English is the language of oil technology and of the people who work in oil . . .") offers the perspective of an oil company employee, Charles Johnson, English Curriculum Specialist at the Arabian American Oil Company (ARAMCO)[2]. His description of

---

[2]The Arabian American Oil Company (ARAMCO) had its origins in 1933 when the Kingdom of Saudi Arabia signed an agreement with Standard Oil Company of California, giving that company exclusive rights to explore, manufacture, and export oil and oil products in the region. In 1936, Texaco became half-owner of what was then the California Arabian Oil Company (CASCO). In 1944, CASCO changed its name to ARAMCO ("History of E Province," 1992). In 1973, Saudi Arabia bought a 25% share in ARAMCO, raising that stake to 60% in 1974 and to 100% in 1988. ("Saudis Reportedly Map," 1988).

English-language teaching in Saudi Arabia shows the extraordinary lengths to which his company went to train non-English speaking employees for company jobs, and leads to the conclusion that dominance of English in technical fields and companies was far from an inevitable or naturally occurring process. It also raises questions about the role of English teachers who are hired to train employees for particular job-related behaviors, tied to specific company needs.

The conference on Adult English for National Development in which Johnson participated took place in Beirut in May 1971. It was sponsored by the Ford Foundation, along with government representatives, academics such as Peter Strevens, Fulbright lecturers, Peace Corps directors, BBC employees, school principals, and employees of other oil companies from various Middle Eastern countries, the United Kingdom, and the United States. The stated purpose of the conference was to extend the services of the American University's Center for English Language Research and Training beyond the university to schools and to private companies in the region, such as banks, airlines, and oil companies. The proceedings reveal that EST research, teaching, and materials, subsidized by governments, industry, and foundations, were geared to meet the needs of industry and to exert Western influence in the area. Johnson's contribution to the proceedings shows a side of ESP not usually discussed in the literature: its role in furthering the economic aims of a company. That is, the training ARAMCO workers underwent included English instruction to foster particular attitudes, behavior, and thinking the company deemed appropriate for its workers, as the following quote from Johnson's conference paper (1971) indicates:

> It is the position of ARAMCO training today that if the course of academic study is to help produce the kind of employee the Company wants and needs, then training must go beyond the imparting of academic learning; it must involve itself in changing attitudes and behaviors, to make a better "achiever." (p. 66).

When describing the training itself, Johnson makes it clear that English is a necessary but insufficient component of ARAMCO's lessons: "English training is only a part—although a very important part—of a larger program designed to make the Saudi an effective member of the ARAMCO workforce" (p. 55). The larger program includes academic courses in "math, general science, physics, chemistry, history, geography, and commercial subjects—all taught in English—as well as English itself" (p. 55). Johnson frames this program as "roughly the equivalent of an 11th grade education in a U.S. high school" (p. 55), an interesting but unexplored reference to a desire to acculturate these workers according to U.S. specifications.

In fact, acculturation, or reculturation, is an explicit goal of the training, yet is presented as a benign and expansive process benefitting the workers and company equally: "The Company does not take the narrow view that training is simply a matter of giving a man the specific skills that are required on his job. Rather it has pursued the long-range goal of developing the man to his maximum potential—and this means educating him in the broader sense. This is in ARAMCO's best interests . . ." (pp. 65–66). To carry out these goals, the curriculum goes beyond teaching subjects to include "a special emphasis on thinking skills" so that the worker can gain a "broad and deeper understanding of the world in which he lives and of his place in it" (p. 66).

The disturbing implication that the Saudi student-workers had a narrow and shallow understanding of the world in which they lived, and their place in it, and therefore needed a U.S. oil company to teach them to think more broadly and deeply is further elaborated by Johnson in his identification of problems encountered in teaching the students. I quote this part of the conference paper (Johnson, 1971) to show the condescending attitude it reveals toward Saudi (non-Western) culture:

> The program, of course, has not been without its problems and challenges. In the teaching of English, for instance, we are not dealing with people who are merely learning another language and culture—as might be the case with Frenchmen, Germans or Russians; rather, we are dealing with people whose education is of a traditional, non-western type. Our learners, whatever their association with the modern world through the Company and through the media, are still largely traditional in outlook. For the most part, they still see themselves as living in a world in which they are subject to forces beyond their control, dependent upon external authority—the family, the tribe, the religion, the government, the Company. (pp. 67–68)

In this and other passages, Johnson associates *modern* and *Western* with superior and *traditional* and *non-Western* with backward. Part of his job, as he sees it, is to modernize Saudis so they can become productive workers. However, the contradiction is that although he claims to want them to think for themselves, to join the *modern* world, as he sees it, he seems to actually want them to think for the company. This contradiction is played out in an example Johnson gives of what he considers to be students' stubborn dependence on external authority. Johnson ascribes a superior cultural position to himself and the other teachers, revealed in his use of *we* to refer to that group, while using *them* to refer to students: "Sometimes when *we* (italics mine) have explained a task and set *them* (italics mine) to work, *they* (italics mine) will write a few words or lines and then come up to the desk: "Is this what you want, teacher?" (p. 68).

According to Johnson, students' requests for help or approval are unacceptable because "the grade [for the assignment] to be meaningful, must depend upon the individual's own achievement; it is not something given to him by the teacher" (p. 68). What Johnson does not acknowledge is that the teachers in this setting *are* the authorities, with grading as their principle instrument of power, as it is in most teaching situations. Students' reliance on teachers' authority is not a cultural artifact but an institutional one. In this case, the institution is a Western oil company. Yet, Johnson seems to expect the impossible: Students should rely on themselves rather than the teacher for feedback and guidance, even though they will eventually be judged by the person they are not supposed to consult. In addition, his remarks about students' dependence on authority are, at best, confusing. He disdains their putative dependence on family, tribe, religion, government, and ARAMCO, but at the same time, he admits that a goal of the training is to "form thinking and study habits more in line with Company needs" (p. 72). It would perhaps have been more honest to concede that the training was supposed to discredit all forms of authority in the students' lives except those connected to the company's needs. That achieved, students'/workers' thinking would be unambivalently aligned with company goals.

Johnson's paper reveals that the ARAMCO training consisted not of courses narrowly focused on English for specific purposes but in assimilation to the company's practices, its focus on carrying out its business, making the workers into company men. Yet, other presenters at the Beirut conference seem to have been comfortable with that goal and willing to lend the ESP imprimatur and their academic credentials to what amounts to an employee-training program with a focus on developing adherence to the needs of private companies. For example, Strevens (1971a), in his conference paper in the same proceedings, "English for Specific Purposes: A Specialist's Viewpoint," offers the services of English teachers to further the goals of the oil industry and other private sector companies in that region. Note that Strevens, like other conference presenters, refers to those in the private and public sector responsible for hiring English teachers as "consumers," thus promoting ESP as a commercial enterprise: "I think the profession can now say that the consumer—for instance, to the oil industry or to a shipping firm, or even to a government—if you, the consumer will describe accurately the precise achievement in English that you require, we can 'engineer' a system that will reach this target with a very small wastage rate" (p. 35). Strevens' (1971a) aim was greater "professionalisation" (p. 48) of ELT by moving from a literature-based curriculum to a more narrowly focused curriculum based on "consumer's" needs:

> The most important single requirement upon the consumer is that he should describe in as much detail as possible just what command of English he is seeking from his employees. To invent an example at the lowest level, suppose an oil company wants to train drilling-rig hands to use English. The company might specify oral English only, with no need to write it and with reading ability restricted to a dozen crucial instructions (like DANGER, EXPLOSIVES,

NO SMOKING) . . . A specification of this kind would make it possible for the language teaching specialist to prepare suitable courses and teaching materials and to predict a high rate of success. (p. 40)

Whereas Strevens envisions ESP as contextualized language teaching, Johnson views ARAMCO's training as the "long-range goal of developing the man to his maximum potential" (pp. 65–66), yet in both these formulations, English-language teaching is commidified. Along with rejection of the traditional exam-driven, literature-based ELT curriculum, which Strevens viewed as "essentially useless for the learner's eventual purpose" (p. 36), there was a concomitant willingness to turn over control to "consumers," trusting their requirements as useful aims of instruction. Overlooked in this shift is the problematic conflation of employers' and learners' needs. An unstated assumption is that what is good for the company is good for the learner, with no consideration of the working conditions or treatment workers might face on the job. Possible conflicts between employer and employee, teacher and student, or members of varying cultures are not acknowledged. There are no mechanisms for balancing target needs and learners' or workers' rights, a point I return to in my discussion of rights analysis in the next chapter.

My intention in discussing the proceedings of the 1971 conference on Adult English for National Development is not to expose the role of a particular company, curriculum specialist, or academic consultant in promoting English around the world but, rather, to show that ESP did not develop inevitably and naturally. The 1971 Beirut conference is just one example of the conscious planning on the part of industry, aided by governments, foundations, and academic institutions working together to shore up markets in developing countries. This is ESP's unofficial history, one that has been ignored in the literature. What gets left out when this history is not discussed are the political and ethical implications of the entire undertaking. ESP was never, nor is it now, purely a language-teaching enterprise but also a political and economic one. The literature's silence on these issues means that more work must be done to explore them. In that spirit, I turn to Phillipson (1992) for further analysis of the field's economic roots.

Phillipson's Analysis of the Political and Economic Roots of English Language Teaching

Chapter 6 of Phillipson's (1992) *Linguistic Imperialism* entitled "British and American Promotion of English" is an important corrective to the ESP literature's portrayal of the "rise" of English worldwide as a natural and politically neutral phenomenon. Phillipson clearly demonstrates that, to the contrary, a coalition of U.K. and U.S. governmental agencies, foundations, industries, and universities worked to promote English-language teaching and publishing for strategic and economic reasons. His account, however, is not a "simplistic conspiracy theory" of closed-door meetings in cigar-filled rooms (p. 151) but, rather, an exploration how political and economic interests guided the conscious promotion of English. To do this, he focuses on the origins and growing influence of the British Council, an agency responsible for much of the funding of ESP teaching, teacher training, and materials development from the mid-1960s to the present. In addition, Phillipson discusses the U.S. promotion of English, including the role of foundations, such as Ford, and the coordinated efforts by the British and U.S. governments to ensure the dominance of English throughout the world.

The British Council's Promotion of English.   According to Phillipson (1992), the British Council's origins can be traced to 1934 when the British Foreign Office, prompted by members of the business community, formed a committee, The British Council for Relations with Other Countries (p. 137), to explore ways to promote English language teaching and British culture abroad. Although funding initially came from private companies, the Foreign Office's contribution rose over the next 50 years, offering a classic case of public monies used to promote the interests of the private sector. In the 30's and 40's, the Foreign Office involved the British Council in activities "designed to combat German and Italian propaganda" (p. 138), such as setting up cultural centers, supporting British schools, donating books, and offering scholarships throughout the Commonwealth and abroad, especially in countries where the Germans and Italians had already made inroads. After the war, the British Council played a greater role in promoting commercial interests due to a "flagging economy" and the need to reduce military spending (p. 144). The English language was seen as an asset that could compensate for the United Kingdom's diminished military strength. Therefore, in the 1950s, plans were drawn up to carry out a more concerted effort to export English and English-language teaching.

The battle to increase the influence of English was fought on three fronts, according to Phillipson: British embassies, the BBC, and the British Council. Two reports published during the 1950s convinced the British cabinet to significantly increase its spending on the promotion of English. The *Drogheda Report,* issued in 1954, outlined a direct relationship among countering Communist influence, building up trade overseas, and "increasing the use of English as the common language in the East" (*Drogheda Report,* 1954, cited in Phillipson, 1992, p. 146). One sentence from that report, quoted by Phillipson, describes in a particularly frank way a cause-and-effect relationship between promoting English and developing new markets: "In the very long term we have no doubt that the work of the British Council, especially in regard to the teaching of English in Asia, will be highly beneficial to our overseas trade" (*Drogheda Report,* 1954, cited in Phillipson, 1992, p. 146). The report was also clear about the need for the

British Council to support English as the *lingua franca* in India, Pakistan, the Far East, and the Middle East, and to secure its position as the language of science and technology.

The second influential report was issued in 1956 by the Official Committee on the Teaching of English Overseas, whose representatives came from government agencies involved in foreign affairs, education, and trade, including the British Council. In it, they declared that "opportunities unquestionably exist for increasing the use of English as the main second language in most parts of the non-English speaking world" (Ministry of Education, 1956, cited in Phillipson, 1992, p. 147). Recommendations for carrying out this goal included increasing the number of British teachers of all subjects overseas, bringing larger numbers of teachers from overseas for training, expanding university courses in British universities to provide that training, and expanding the role of the BBC in teaching English through the radio. Another recommendation was to bolster the role of the British Council in overseas facilities for training teachers of English by providing more government funding for these projects. Publication was another area where the report offered suggestions, including a greater role for the British Council in working with authors and private publishers to produce more British textbooks, in part to counter the growing incursion of U.S. publishers in overseas markets. Finally, the report supported plans, initiated by the British Council "with the backing of the Foreign Office, Commonwealth Relations Office, and the Colonial Office" (p. 150), for a new department of EFL at the University of Edinburgh. It is interesting to note that this department was where several prominent ESP scholars, including Martin Bates and Tim Johns (Dudley-Evans, personal communication, December 1999) got their training. The British government responded positively to both reports, increasing the British Council's budget significantly during the 1950s.

U.S. Promotion of English. One distinction, made by Phillipson, between U.S. and U.K. promotion of English worldwide is the important role of private foundations, such as the Ford Foundation, in promoting the business interests of the "American power elite" (p. 154), members of which serve as trustees of these foundations. This is not to say that the U.S. government was uninvolved in promoting English. To the contrary, "[n]o fewer than six government agencies were involved in English-teaching activities" (p. 158): the State Department, which funded the Fulbright program; the Agency for International Development; the U.S. Office of Education; the Defense Department; the Peace Corps; and, the Department of the Interior. Among these activities were radio broadcasts, libraries, language courses, academic exchanges, and cultural exchanges. Phillipson shows that U.S. aid to other countries is unapologetically justified as a way to further U.S. foreign policy aims, as this quote he offers from a 1983 policy review issued by the Commission on Security and

Economic Assistance shows: "[A] judicious use of foreign assistance tools can optimize U.S. influence and contribute importantly to the success of American foreign policy"(cited in Phillipson, 1992, p. 158).

Getting back to private foundations, Phillipson discusses their role in "establishing ESL as an academic discipline" (pp. 160–161), including creating universities in areas of strategic importance to the U.S.; teacher training projects; curriculum development projects; funding of overseas students to train in U.S. universities; and training U.S. citizens as overseas consultants. Of special interest to ESP's unofficial history, is the Ford Foundation's involvement with the British Council in planning the University of Edinburgh's School of Applied Linguistics, a training ground for ESP experts. In addition, the Ford Foundation had English-language teaching projects in 38 countries by the mid-1960s (p. 161) and as I showed in the previous section, funded ESP conferences where the interests of private industry were the driving force. The Ford Foundation also helped fund the Center for Applied Linguistics (CAL).

Phillipson discusses other coordinated efforts by the United Kingdom and the United States, in addition to the University of Edinburgh's School of Applied Linguistics, to promote English and English language teaching, including conferences in 1955, 1959 and 1961, in which British Council staff met with United States Information Agency (USIA) and CAL staff to formulate joint policy statements and develop strategies for implementation of projects. Phillipson underscores the political nature of the conference participants' work. They saw English as a tool for fighting Communism and believed that those who learned English would be turning toward the future rather than remaining stuck in what they characterized as traditional or nationalistic thinking. Yet, conference participants did not acknowledge their jobs as political, despite ties of English-language teaching worldwide to foreign policy objectives of their respective countries. They did not seem to question plans to use English as a tool to change the thinking and loyalties of citizens in countries where English was being taught. Instead, they saw English as a ticket to the modern world.

Phillipson's work documents the dominance of English as the result of successful planning on the part of various interests in the United Kingdom and United States. He shows that English-language teaching is a political activity. Yet, he explains, ELT is guided by an "ideology of political purity," (p. 165), a phrase I elaborate on in the next chapter in a section on the ideology of EAP.

SUMMARY

EAP's discourse of neutrality has presented the history of this field as a consensual and inevitable chronology of pedagogical events rather than a well-crafted and organized effort on the part of governments, businesses, and foundations working together to promote English language teaching, conferences, publications, and faculty exchanges, ensuring that markets and labor would be available to promote their economic interests.

Why is it important to acknowledge the economic roots and ideological underpinnings of EAP? Because without that understanding, those working in it will be operating under naive assumptions about the English language (e.g., it is neutral), English language teaching (e.g., it grew inevitably because of increased demand by learners), and learning (e.g., students want English unambivalently). A critical approach to EAP avoids these uncomplicated and ahistorical assumptions and allows for a more nuanced and dynamic relationship between target situations and students' purposes, desires, and aspirations.

Yet, I am clearly not advocating a return to English for general purposes; rather I endorse EAP's attempts to examine the reasons why students are enrolled in English courses and how their goals relate to the types of courses they will take as they pursue degrees in their chosen areas of study. I applaud EAP's responsiveness to specific institutional demands, academic requirements, and classroom activities. Still, I hope this book offers an alternative to EAP as a service enterprise, offered up unconditionally to public- and private-sector programs to ensure that their target goals are met. Instead, EAP professionals can begin to theorize an ethics of their practice, making decisions about which projects to involve themselves in, based on information about funding, goals, and possible outcomes for students. These issues are explored more fully in the examples of critical EAP in Part II.

Chapter 3

Debating EAP Issues: Pedagogy and Ideology

This chapter presents two major debates about EAP that have emerged in the last two decades. Each critique of EAP is followed by a discussion of the published responses to it in the EAP literature. The first debate is between L2 compositionists and EAP specialists, centering on what should and should not be taught to non-native speakers of English, especially those enrolled in ESL university writing classes in anglophone countries. It is an exchange about the most appropriate pedagogy and content for postsecondary composition courses. The second debate revolves around ideology, that is, the political implications of EAP's pragmatic approach to research and teaching. One purpose of discussing these debates is to demonstrate that EAP is a contested field in which openness to questions raised by critics strengthens its theory and practice. The other is to set the stage for chapter 4, where I outline a theory of critical EAP.

L2 COMPOSITIONISTS' CRITIQUE

ESL compositionists Raimes (1991a, 1991b), Spack (1988), and Zamel (1993, 1995) question EAP's premise that ESL college instruction should be guided by the specific demands of academic content courses. Instead, they view ESL writing courses as places where students can become better writers no matter what personal, academic, professional, or rhetorical situation they might encounter. That is, they favor general over specific English language teaching. In addition, they oppose EAP's reliance on academic genres as models of writing, believing that literary texts along with a variety of nonacademic articles and documents serve as better models for student writers. For these authors, then, ESL composition is a liberal arts course, part of students' formation in the humanities, preparation for an uncertain future.

Raimes (1991b), for example, rejects the position of ESL as a service to college content courses. Instead, she views ESL composition as a humanities course in a liberal arts curriculum with an "intrinsic subject matter" (p. 243): grammar, literature, and culture. Raimes therefore rejects proposals for offering "modules of marketing, accounting, and nursing" to the immigrant first-year students at the U.S. publicly funded college in which she teaches, viewing these as a departure from "the very tradition of a liberal arts education" (p. 420). So, while acknowledging that ESP might be appropriate for international graduate students, she believes that the students she teaches, "need general English" (p. 420).

Spack (1988), too, argues for English for general academic purposes based on her belief that neither L1 nor L2 writing teachers should be expected to teach genres of academic disciplines to which they do not belong: "The best we can accomplish is to create programs in which students can learn general inquiry strategies, rhetorical principles, and tasks that can transfer to other course work" (pp. 40–41). General writing courses avoid the problem of recruiting writing teachers to work outside their own discipline, an enterprise Spack finds problematic for two reasons. First, they "lack control over content" (p. 37) in other disciplines and therefore do a disservice to those disciplines, the students, and themselves when they attempt to teach their genres. Second, writing teachers should teach "the academic writing process," that is, "appropriate inquiry strategies, planning, drafting, consulting, revising, and editing" (p. 45). The academic writing process is writing teachers' area of expertise and should therefore be their focus of instruction, according to Spack.

Spack (1988) outlines a number of ways to teach writing to ESL undergraduates "without the need for linking courses with another subject-area program" (p. 41). These suggestions are grounded in two skills, working with data and writing from other texts, Spack claims are common to all types of academic writing. The rationale for working on these skills is that they are "transferable to many writing tasks that students will be required to perform in other courses when they write for academic audiences" (p. 44). The concentration on transferable skills and writing process, she believes, will prepare students to write in future academic courses, whatever the subject matter or formal constraints. It will also reassert the place of English composition as a "humanities course: A place where students are provided the enrichment of reading and writing that provoke thought and foster their intellectual and ethical development" (p. 46).

Zamel (1993, 1995) takes a similar position in arguing for general academic writing skills rather than specific genres. Having reviewed L1 studies on writing across the disciplines and interviewed ESL students enrolled in various content courses, she recommends teaching English for general rather than specific purposes, based on the following conclusions:

1. students will encounter a variety of unpredictable assignments in their future courses;
2. their interpretations of those assignments will be unique and idiosyncratic; and
3. their academic coursework will be "generally unimaginative and formulaic" (Zamel, 1993, p. 34), with the subject matter presented in an "authoritarian" manner, preventing students from "engaging with material and work they are assigned." (Zamel, 1993, p. 34).

Due to these assumptions, Zamel (1993) finds EAP to be based on unreliable and unworthy models of ESL writing instruction. The alternative she proposes is to teach the common features of all discourses, those that "transcend all boundaries," especially those "features that characterize all 'good writing'" rather than the "presumable differences" (p. 35). Zamel (1993) offers examples of what she considers to be good writing when describing assignments from her thematic writing courses that call on students to read and write about historical documents, court decisions, newspaper accounts, fiction, poetry, and biographies:

> Through all this work, I invited students' reactions, their analyses and interpretations, their attempts to use new concepts and language, and urged them to make connections between this work and their own experiences and assumptions . . . [this work] generated rich, compelling, and memorable pieces that reflected the questions and issues students were grappling with, their active engagement with the material, their use of the material to think about the world around them, to think about the ways in which this material and their world intersect, to think about their thinking. (p. 37)

It is this type of intellectually engaging writing Zamel (1993, 1995) would like to see not just in ESL writing courses but across the curriculum. To achieve this aim, she proposes conducting workshops with colleagues in other disciplines and encouraging alternative assessments, such as portfolios. However, she does not recommend linked courses as a way to foster cross-curricular collaboration.

The opposition of Raimes (1991a, 1991b), Spack (1988), and Zamel (1993, 1995) to linked courses is due in part to concerns about the subordination of ESL faculty to the colleagues with whom they coordinate instruction, what Raimes (1991b) calls "the butler's stance" (p. 243). In this conceptualization of linked courses, the ESL course serves the needs of the content courses rather than participating in an arrangement where both parties contribute and influence each other equally. These concerns are understandable, given the lack of reciprocity apparent in most descriptions of linked courses in the EAP literature; the majority are at the low end of Barron's (1992) "co-operative continuum," discussed in chapter 1. However, as I show in chapter 4, on a theory of critical EAP, and in the examples of linked courses in the second part of the book, ESL faculty and students do not have to position themselves as compliant objects in the relationship. They can instead participate as active subjects, influencing the content class rather than passively submitting to its requirements.

RESPONSES TO L2 COMPOSITIONISTS' CRITIQUE

Of the publications critiquing the aims and methods of EAP, Spack's (1988), "Initiating ESL students into the academic discourse community: How far should we go?" has received the most attention. Those who responded, in the TESOL Quarterly (Braine, 1988; Johns, 1988b) and in other books and articles, have generally taken the opportunity to clarify their positions and reassert their goals. Dudley-Evans and St. John (1998), for example, agree with Spack (1988) that academic genres across disciplines share certain discoursal features. However, finding enough differences across genres to merit the level of specificity called for in ESP, they reject Spack's call for teaching English for general academic purposes and reiterate the importance of content-specific teaching ". . . if we are to meet our students' needs we must deal with subject-specific matters. Our case is that subject-specific work needs to be into specific disciplines rather than into broad disciplinary areas" (p. 51).

Johns (1988b) believes that Spack's (1988) rejection of linked courses is a regressive move, a refusal to join the "academic fray" (p. 706) at a time of cross-curricular experimentation, especially in U.S. universities, leading to interesting collaborations and research. She also raises the concern that teaching general reading and writing tasks, as Spack recommends, would leave ESL students without the tools to face the "specific demands of the target culture" and "understand various professors as audiences" (p. 706). Rather than "retreat[ing] into our classrooms and teach[ing] what we already know," a reference to Spack's position of maintaining the boundaries between ESL and other disciplines, Johns (1997) recommends that ESL teachers call upon their "unique abilities to explore academic worlds: their language; their genres; their values, and their literacies, remembering at all times that these worlds are complex and evolving, conflicted and messy" (p. 154). Her aim is to offer students opportunities to carry out this type of research across the disciplines "to explore, investigate, and critique their current and future communities of practice" (p. 154).

Swales (1990) shares Johns' view of ESP as a way to make students aware of the centrality of discourse through discussions of "prototypical examples of relevant genres" (p. 215) so that they can adjust themselves to the demands of various discourse communities. He dismisses but does not directly address Spack's (1988) concern about English teachers attempting to teach content outside of their discipline. Instead, he offers a rationale for genre-based ESP based on professional concerns. That is, whereas Raimes (1991a, 1991b), Spack (1988) and Zamel (1993, 1995)

assert that the status of ESL instruction in universities can be elevated only
if it has a liberal-arts focus with no direct ties to other disciplines, Swales
accepts ESL as a service function in higher education, one he believes is
necessary even though, he acknowledges, it relegates ESL teachers to the
bottom of the academic ladder.

To elevate ESL teaching, he suggests carrying out genre analysis, "an
escape from the ivory ghetto of remediation" (p. 11). Studying "senior"
genres, such as the research article, is "one of the more rewarding ways of
winning friends and having influence in higher places" (p. 11). So, the
rationale for studying and teaching "research-process" genres is not
only to benefit students but also to gain the recognition of colleagues in
more prestigious departments. This is preferable to remaining on the
bottom rung of the academic ladder where general English language
teaching is situated: "There is much anecdotal evidence to suggest that
colleagues from other discourse communities are both surprised and
impressed when the English instructor arrives armed with lines of
inquiry that show sensitivity to possible pressures on that community's
central genres" (p. 216).

The views of Raimes (1991a, 1991b), Spack (1988), and Zamel (1993,
1995), and those of Swales (1990), although pedagogically different, share
a common ideology: None offers proposals for challenging the inequities
on which academic hierarchies are founded. By insisting that ESL
composition is an equal partner with other disciplines and can therefore
coexist without relating to them directly, the L2 compositionists do not
address the power differential. For his part, Swales (1990) acknowledges
the unequal position of ESL and other disciplines and tries to transcend
the low status of ESL by appealing to better-placed colleagues. The
options offered by their responses to academic hierarchies are to ignore
them or to ascend them. Other possible responses are presented in the
following section and next chapter.

One other similarity in the positions of the L2 compositionists and the
ESP specialists is that both are predicated on a belief in skills transfer. The
first group believes that general writing skills transfer to future writing
assignments. The second group claims that teaching genres will prepare
students for their future academic classes: "If we can make genres the class
focus and teach variety and openness to texts, we may more appropriately
prepare students for the demands of academic classrooms and their
professional lives" (Johns, 1995, p. 289). Yet, the research of Prior (1995)
and Leki (1995), raises doubts about these claims and points to the need
for further classroom-initiated research along the lines proposed by
McDonough (1986) to develop EAP's research base. The case studies of
linked classes in Part II of this book are in part a response to the call for
participatory research grounded in classroom practices and students'
responses.

CRITICAL THEORISTS'[3] CRITIQUE

EAP's Ideology of Pragmatism

Where Phillipson (1992) has raised concerns about ELT's "ideology of political purity," discussed in chapter 2, I have problematized EAP's "ideology of pragmatism" (Benesch, 1993). Both labels question the political quietism of the literature investigated and highlight the need to discuss the politics of teaching, including funding, curricular choices, roles ascribed to teachers and students, and the goals of English teaching in institutions and societies. My critique of EAP's ideology of pragmatism is directed at its assumption that students should accommodate themselves to the demands of academic assignments, behaviors expected in academic classes, and hierarchical arrangements within academic institutions. In addition, EAP's pragmatism assumes ESL faculty should subordinate their instruction to those demands, behaviors, and arrangements, perpetuating a service relationship to colleagues in other departments. The accommodation of EAP students and faculty is rationalized by appeals to "realism" and "authenticity" (Johns, 1990b; Reid, 1989). Reid (1989), for example, argues that ESL composition teachers should be "pragmatists," who "discover what will be expected in the academic contexts their students will encounter" and "provide their students with the writing skills and cultural information that will allow their students to perform successfully" (p. 232). This one-sided arrangement of the EAP teacher studying the writing activities and cultural demands of content classes and teaching them to students ensures that the academic status quo will be upheld. The EAP teacher is not expected to question the pedagogical or intellectual soundness of the activities observed. They take place in content classes and are therefore considered a "realistic" and "appropriate" basis for EAP instruction (Horowitz, 1986b, p. 447).

On the surface it would seem that my critique of EAP is the same as the L2 compositionists'. Like them, I question EAP's slavish devotion to content course demands and the subordinate role of ESL teachers in linked and content-based courses. However, I do not support their position to maintain the boundaries between ESL and other disciplines nor the emphasis on literary texts and documents deemed to be models of "good" writing. On this point, I agree with Johns (1988b) that the refusal to join the "academic fray" (p. 706) is a lost opportunity for cross-curricular research and collaboration, but, unlike Johns, my support for joining the academic fray is not to base my EAP courses on the "linguistic and cultural demands of authentic university classes" (p. 706), as she recommends. Rather, I find linked courses to be an effective vehicle for EAP faculty and students to influence and possibly change conditions in academic culture, by providing opportunities to interact directly with the teachers, curricula, texts, and

---

[3]I include my work in this section, considering it critical theory (and practice).

instruction students encounter as they earn degrees. When they participate directly with content courses, EAP faculty witness what goes on and can work with students to improve conditions.

This does not mean that I see EAP solely as a tool for academic and social transformation. Certainly, it has a pragmatic function to perform. However, that pragmatism need not be "vulgar" but can instead be "critical," a distinction made by Cherryholmes (1988)[4] and applied by Pennycook (1997) to his discussion of EAP's pragmatism (summarized later in this chapter).

Needs Analysis in EAP

Target Needs and Learner Needs. There is concensus in the EAP literature about the centrality of needs analysis. For example, according to Dudley-Evans and St. John (1998), "needs analysis is the cornerstone of ESP and leads to a very focused course" (p. 122). Jordan (1997) proposes that needs analysis should be the "starting point for devising syllabuses, courses, materials, and the kind of teaching and learning that takes place" (p. 22). Robinson (1991) does acknowledge that needs analysis is influenced by "the ideological preconceptions of the analysts" (p. 7), but ways in which ideology permeates needs analysis is not taken up by Robinson or other EAP specialists. Addressing this question is one of my overarching goals in this section and the book as a whole.

In the early years of EAP, needs were associated strictly with target situation demands. More recently, due in part to Hutchinson and Waters (1987, p. 54), distinctions are made between *target situation needs* ("what the learner needs to do in the target situation") and *learning needs* ("what the learner needs to do in order to learn"). These authors break target needs down further, into three categories: *necessities, lacks,* and *wants. Necessities* are "what the learner has to know in order to function effectively in the target situation" (p. 55); *lacks* are the "necessities the learner lacks" (p. 56); *wants* "what the learners want or feel they need" (p. 57). In making these distinctions, Hutchinson and Waters question the exclusive focus on external requirements of needs analysis in early EAP. They stress the importance of attending to learning and the possibility of a mismatch between institutional demands and learners' perceptions of what they need. However, despite the increased sophistication of this type of needs analysis, it nonetheless aims to fulfill target expectations without questioning them. That is, while taking learning into account, this type of needs analysis accepts target goals as immutable. Hutchinson and Waters describe the ESP

---

[4]Although he has since revised his views on the distinction between vulgar and critical pragmatism, Cherryholmes (1999) recalls his earlier formulation of vulgar pragmatism as "something bounded by a horizon of immediacy," work that is "crass, expedient, and short-sighted" (p. 7).

course as a journey whose destination (target needs) is known, but the route (learning needs) has yet to be discovered. Analyzing learning needs is a way to determine the route which, the authors hope, will be interesting, enjoyable and engaging while at the same time "maintain[ing] its relevance to target needs" (p. 93).

Missing from Hutchinson and Waters' (1987) formulation is any notion that target needs are subject to criticism or change. Their position is that "[s]ociety sets the target (in the case of ESP, performance in the target situation) and the individuals must do their best to get as close to that target as possible (or reject it)" (p. 72). How the target might be rejected is not explored. Instead, the "determining influence" (p. 72) of the target is elaborated. Nor do Hutchinson and Waters explain their idea that "society" sets target needs. Instead, that abstraction is accepted as a given, something that cannot be negotiated (Who could negotiate with "society"?) Yet, as Phillipson's (1992) research, discussed in the previous chapter, shows, what might be labeled "society" is far from abstract, but rather consists of people working for governments, businesses, and foundations who promote their interests with particular outcomes in mind. Therefore, I argue, to arrive at an ethics of EAP, needs analysis must include examination of who sets the goals, why they were formulated, whose interests are served by them, and whether they should be challenged. In order to carry out this type of investigation, needs analysis must be critical as well as pragmatic.

Critical Needs Analysis.   To illustrate *critical needs analysis*, I offer an example from my teaching where I raised questions about target goals rather than assuming they should be the sole determinant of my instruction (Benesch, 1996). The EAP writing class for which I was developing a syllabus was linked to a 450-student psychology lecture class taught by two faculty members from the psychology department. Critical needs analysis revealed that the target needs were not a unified set of goals or a clear destination for my EAP class to reach but, rather, requirements from different levels of the academic hierarchy, some of which were contradictory. For example, at the highest level of the hierarchy, the university level, all students were required to pass a 50-minute argumentative essay exam to continue on to first-year composition, a prerequisite for further study and a requirement for graduation. According to this target need, I should have been working with my students to prepare for that exam by practicing essays in which they took a side on a social issue and argued that position with supporting examples. At a lower level of the hierarchy, the psychology department, was the psychology class, a 3-hour-a-week lecture in a poorly lit auditorium where students listened, took notes, and were prepared for multiple-choice tests. The target needs in this course required a different type of EAP instruction: reviewing lectures notes, discussing textbook material, and studying for tests. The relationship between these different sets of goals, established at different levels of the university, writing essays on the one hand, and understanding lecture and textbook material on the other, presented a challenge for the EAP syllabus. Adding to the difficulty was the fact that the psychology professors wanted the students to apply the lecture and textbook material to their daily lives, although budget cuts had eliminated discussion sections in which those types of connections would normally have been explored. So, the EAP course was seen by the psychology department as a place where discussions linking psychological concepts and personal experience would take place. Because I have written about this class elsewhere (Benesch, 1996), I will not discuss here ways I addressed these contradictory demands. Instead, I turn to how I addressed needs that did not originate directly in response to the target but, instead, from my goal of offering students a critical alternative to the psychology course pedagogy and syllabus.

Critical needs analysis was a way to find areas where some of the target needs might be supplemented and modified. Unhappy with the one-way flow of information from the psychology faculty to the students in the lecture class, I made two proposals to the faculty about ways to promote greater dialogue; they responded enthusiastically to both. The first was for them to use questions my students wrote in the EAP class about lecture or textbook material as the basis for part of a subsequent lecture; the other was for one of the two faculty to visit my class for a more immediate and personal interaction with the 15 EAP students in their course. As it turned out, the first activity did not succeed in promoting greater dialogue because even though the EAP students' questions were answered by the psychology professors, there was no chance for further discussion given the size of the lecture class. The second activity did achieve the type of interaction the students were hoping for and, in fact, one student wrote in her feedback about the psychology professor's visit that she preferred the smaller class to the lecture and hoped the professor would return to the EAP class "to teach us again":

> I learned more than I did in the lecture class because I'm able to ask him questions face to face instead of yelling out in the big class ... In conclusion, I really like the way he teaching the class which consists of lot of outside information and experiences. Also I was truly benefitted by his clear and deep explanations. I hope that he would have more chances to teach us again (student text, cited in Benesch, 1996, p. 734)

Another intervention on my part was to supplement the masculinist curriculum of the psychology course (the contributions of women psychologists were not discussed) with a research project in the EAP class on the topic of anorexia (see chapter 5).

Rights Analysis. The term *needs analysis* has always struck me as inadequate for a process fraught with ambiguity, struggle, and contradiction. By offering *critical needs analysis*, I had hoped to underscore the political nature of syllabus design in EAP. Yet, I was uneasy with retaining *needs*, a word that seems more related to biological processes (e.g., need for food, sleep, shelter, etc.) or psychological ones, and not appropriate for the social processes related to education. Most objectionable is *learner needs*, a term conflating institutional demands and students' needs. Searching for a way to convey how power struggles are embedded in educational decision-making, I have replaced *critical needs analysis* with *rights analysis*. This allows for a two-pronged strategy of addressing target needs, through traditional needs analysis, and exploring possibilities for changing them, through *rights analysis* (Benesch, 1999a). Juxtaposing *needs analysis* and *rights analysis* allows for two different types of research. The first is a way to discover and perhaps fulfill target goals; the second is a search for alternatives to strict adherence to those requirements. In the next chapter on critical EAP, I explore *rights analysis* further, including its deliberately political connotation and its relationship to language rights and civil rights. For now, I turn to Pennycook's discussion of critical pragmatism, another way to consider both recognizing and challenging target demands.

Critical Pragmatism

Pennycook (1997) suggests Cherryholmes' (1988) distinction between *vulgar pragmatism* and *critical pragmatism* as a way to conceptualize the ideological differences between EAP accepting and promoting target goals and EAP recognizing these goals but perhaps aiming to challenge them. According to Pennycook, EAP has mainly been driven by vulgar pragmatism because of the "discourses of neutrality" (p. 256) guiding its research and practice. By discourses of neutrality, he is referring to certain assumptions underlying EAP: English is a neutral language; language in general is neutral; science and technology are neutral rather than cultural and social; academic institutions are neutral places rather than sites of struggle between competing interests. Pennycook claims that these discourses of neutrality prevent EAP from having the language to reveal its politics. Instead, its goals and activities are presented as inevitable and natural.

To illustrate how "discourses of neutrality . . . help construct EAP as a pragmatic enterprise" (p. 257), Pennycook (1997) deconstructs the term *English for academic purposes* itself. He points out that the *for* connecting *English* and *academic purposes* reveals "a particular view of language as a neutral medium through which meanings pass" (p. 257). He argues that this instrumental or functional view of language obscures the social, cultural, and ideological contexts of language "as always engaged in how we understand the world" (p. 258). English *for* academic purposes, then, constructs an "unproblematic relationship between English and academic purposes" (p. 257), lending itself to vulgar pragmatism, accepting the conditions observed and reproducing them as efficiently as possible.

Critical pragmatism, on the other hand, involves continually evaluating those conditions and making "epistemological, ethical, and aesthetic choices . . . and translating them into discourse-practices" (Cherryholmes, 1988, quoted in Pennycook, 1997, p. 256). Critical EAP, then, involves not only scrutinizing target goals but also ELT's own position in academic culture. This stance avoids a service role for EAP classes, repositioning them "not as mere adjuncts to the knowledge curricula but rather as sites of change and resistance" (p. 263). The EAP classes discussed in Part II of this book are examples of ELT as a site of change and resistance, yet grounded in the practicalities of content-course objectives. That is, they are examples of critical pragmatism, shuttling back and forth between needs analysis and rights analysis, making decisions with students about how to proceed.

RESPONSES TO CRITICAL THEORISTS

One objection to critical theory in EAP has been that discussions of politics and ideology could overwhelm the field, shutting out other theories and approaches. This view is reflected in Allison's response to an article I published in the *TESOL Quarterly* titled "ESL, Ideology and the Politics of Pragmatism" (Benesch, 1993). That article was a reaction to Santos' (1992) characterization of L1 composition as ideological and L2 composition as pragmatic. My aim was to demonstrate that all teaching is ideological, whether or not the politics are acknowledged. I went on to discuss EAP's ideology of pragmatism and to propose a critical alternative to EAP's tradition of unconditionally accepting the findings of needs analysis.

In his response to that article, Allison (1994) labeled my discourse "ideologist" (p. 618) and warned readers that it has a colonizing effect. That is, according to Allison, so-called ideologist discourse is imperialistic; it tries to dominate and hold all other orientations and viewpoints hostage. Allison even expresses reluctance to respond to my article because he believes that in doing so, he is forced to adopt a discourse he finds objectionable:

> As a pragmatically-inclined EAP practitioner, I choose to resist what I see as a current bid on the part of ideologist discourse to invade EAP discourse. I cannot therefore ignore that bid, nor can I afford to debate extensively on ideologist terrain as such participation already entails acceptance of a metaideological agenda. (Allison, 1994, p. 618)

In a later article, Allison (1996) disputes the claim that pragmatism is an ideology, preferring to view it as a "context-sensitive approach" (p. 87), taking into account both "possibilities and constraints that affect what can be achieved and at what cost" (p. 86).

Although I disagree with Allison that critical theorists are interested in colonizing other viewpoints or imposing a single way of thinking on students, I believe his concern is in part a reaction to what I see in retrospect as broad-brush language that blurs important details. For example, in the article on the ideology of pragmatism, I characterize EAP as "accommodationist" (Benesch, 1993, p. 706), in one stroke dismissing the delicate political battles EAP teachers have had to wage in their institutions to gain contextualized language instruction for their students. My genuine regard for EAP appeared to Allison as condescension perhaps because I did not acknowledge the struggles it faces in developing better programs for NNS students in a variety of academic institutions. I hope this book demonstrates my appreciation for the pragmatic side of EAP, even though I propose a more explicit reckoning of its politics and a critical alternative to needs analysis.

Despite my agreement with Allison that critical EAP should avoid sweeping indictments of earlier research, I nonetheless believe that EAP is accountable for having ignored and in most cases, continuing to ignore, issues of power and social justice, leading Santos (1992) to point to a lack of interest in politics in L2 teaching. For example, Allison's construction of EAP students as novices is something that he is not prepared to problematize, a point made clear when he defends EAP's goal of "help[ing] incoming students (starting out as *academic outsiders* [emphasis mine]) to develop an understanding of what academic communication is like and how it operates" (p. 90). This view of academic discourse as a form of communication into which EAP students must be initiated suggests a monologic understanding of learning, with teacher-insiders expecting student-outsiders to adopt their language. Additionally, by presenting academic discourse monolithically, it overlooks the contested nature of knowledge in and outside the academy (Geisler, 1994). It is these types of oversights critical EAP seeks to address. Fortunately, there are examples in the EAP literature of interest in these issues, such as Master (1998), discussed in chapter 4, and Dudley-Evans and St. John (1998), whose consideration of a critical perspective, although with certain caveats, I turn to now.

Dudley-Evans and St. John (1998) include an epilogue to their book, *Developments in English for Specific Purposes: A Multi-Disciplinary Approach,* in which they discuss the undertheorization of ESP throughout its 30 to 40 year history. While applauding its groundedness, through needs analysis, in challenges students face, they regret the "non-theoretical 'here we go' attitude" (p. 230) that has characterized the field. This stance, they state, has contributed to ESP's marginalization in the academy, hindering its "professionalization as a self-standing field" (p. 230). To correct this problem, the authors propose greater attention to issues previously overlooked, "such as gender issues, controversies in Second Language Acquisition, and issues of learners' rights" (p. 230). That is, they have invited the ESP community to engage with heretofore hidden conflicts.

Yet, at the same time, they express trepidation about opening up the field in this way. That is, while welcoming debate about the role of ESP within institutions and agreeing that ESP should not just teach academic requirements, but also interrogate them, they worry that critical approaches might take a "confrontational stance toward current discourse practices" (p. 231). This ambivalence about critical teaching leads the authors to wonder "how far we should go in questioning practices in departments and institutions" (p. 232).

This question posed by Dudley-Evans and St. John (1998) is at the center of critical EAP. How far it should go in challenging academic discourse, assignments and practices is an ongoing issue but one that can be addressed only in the context of particular settings. The examples I offer in Part II of the book show that in some cases students were able to make changes with no negative consequences. In other cases, they gauged that the constraints were too great to attempt any modifications. In others, they were satisfied with current conditions. Yet, whatever the choices and outcomes, critical EAP offered opportunities to question the status quo, an option not usually presented to students in traditional EAP settings. What is clear is that "how far we should go" depends in large part on students' reactions to opportunities critical EAP makes available.

SUMMARY

In this chapter, I have presented debates between EAP specialists and critics from outside the field to show that its pedagogy and politics are areas of contestation and struggle. Although the discourse of consensus in the EAP literature has tended to neutralize contested issues, the debates emerging over the last 20 years about EAP research and practice, from inside and outside the field, show that it is not immune to politics. Highlighting these debates demonstrates EAP's vibrancy, its responsiveness to outsiders' critiques, its own self-scrutiny (Master, 1998), and its openness to change, including increased consideration of academic and social complexities.

Chapter 4

Critical EAP:
Theoretical Influences

Having discussed the official and unofficial histories of EAP and debates about its pedagogy and politics in the three previous chapters, I now turn to a fuller exploration of a theory of critical EAP. Because subsequent chapters offer examples of critical EAP in particular classroom settings, it is important to discuss the theoretical assumptions underlying that practice in this chapter.

The three main influences on my proposals for critical EAP (Benesch, 1993, 1996, 1999a, 1996b) are the theories of Paulo Freire and Michel Foucault and feminist writers, such as Kathleen Weiler, Carmen Luke, and Jennifer Gore, who have added dimensions to critical theory overlooked by male critical theorists. Ways these writers have informed critical EAP are discussed in the first part of the chapter, including similarities and differences in their views. The relationship between traditional EAP and critical EAP is then taken up, through a comparison of needs analysis and rights analysis.

FREIRE: HOPE AND DIALOGUE

My thinking about the limitations of traditional EAP and the promise of a critical approach has been influenced by Freire (1970, 1973, 1994, 1996, 1998a, 1998b). Several central tenets of his pedagogical theories have guided me in considering how to conceptualize and enact critical EAP: hope; limit-situation; untested feasibility; dialogue; and situatedness. These terms are discussed next, as they relate to Freirean pedagogy and critical EAP. Of them all, Freire's concept of hope is the one that distinguishes traditional and critical EAP most clearly, and I therefore begin with a discussion of hope as a defining principle of Freirean pedagogy.

Hope, Limit-Situation, and Untested Feasibility

Freire's (1970) *Pedagogy of the Oppressed* is his best-known book. Twenty years after its appearance, Freire (1994) wrote *Pedagogy of Hope: Reliving Pedagogy of the Oppressed* in which he chronicles the events shaping the first book and renews his commitments to its ideas. In explaining his choice of hope as a frame to revisit the writing and themes of the earlier book, Freire (1994) insists that education is a struggle to improve human existence, not a set of techniques to carry out institutional goals. Unjust and dehumanizing situations offer opportunities to either accept current conditions or challenge them, guided by hope that equitable social arrangements can be achieved. For Freire, education without hope is a journey of despair and inaction. Teachers can train students to resign themselves to the conditions they encounter, no matter how irrational and unjust. Or they can lead their students to "the incessant pursuit of the humanity denied by injustice" through hope and action (Freire, 1970, pp. 72–73). To be human, according to Freire, is to struggle with the tension between good and evil, decency and indecency; that is, to be involved in a political struggle. Education is political and ethical, allowing students and teachers to engage with the conflict between hopelessness and hope: ". . . though I know that things can get worse, I also know that I am able to intervene to improve them" (Freire 1998b, p. 53).

Two terms Freire originally proposed in *Pedagogy of the Oppressed* highlight the ethical and political meanings Freire assigns to *hope: limit-situation* and *untested feasibility*. A *limit-situation* is a personal or political obstacle perceived by humans to restrict their freedom and their ability to carry out their goals. They can either succumb passively to the limitations or resist them. To challenge a limit-situation requires a sense of hope and confidence; submission to its restrictions is an act of hopelessness. The process undertaken to challenge limit-situations is not clearly delineated a priori. Instead, it must be discovered through *limit-acts*, "the defeat and rejection of the given, of a docile, passive acceptance of what is 'there'" (Araujo Freire, 1994, p. 205). The unknown outcome of limit-acts is *untested feasibility*, "something not yet clearly known and experienced, but dreamed of" (p. 207). The dream is enacted when the limit-situation is confronted and transcended, that is when "the untested feasible is no longer merely itself, but has become the concretization of that which within it had previously been infeasible" (p. 207).

Freire's explicitly political and ethical pedagogy and his commitment to liberation and utopia is far from traditional EAP's ideology of pragmatism (Benesch, 1993). In fact, Freire (1994) dismisses pragmatism in the first sentences of *Pedagogy of Hope*, declaring that its discourse encourages resignation and accommodation to the status quo. He allies himself, instead, with the dream of a more humane and democratic future:

> We are surrounded by a pragmatic discourse that would have us adapt to the facts of reality. *Dream* and *utopia*, are called not only useless, but positively impeding. (After all, they are an intrinsic part of any educational practice with the power to unmask the dominant lies) . . . But for me, on the contrary, the educational practice of a progressive option will never be anything but an adventure in unveiling. (p. 7)

Elsewhere Freire (1996) argues that the pragmatic discourse of capitalism serves to paper over conflicts and antagonisms whose appearance might interfere with the smooth promotion of dominant interests. Above all, pragmatism, an "astute ideology," allows for a "focus on production without any preoccupation about what we are producing, who it benefits, or who it hurts" (Freire, 1996, p. 84). Clearly, pragmatism is not neutral but rather is an ideology that hides injustice and inequality in endorsing business as usual (Benesch, 1993).

How can Freire's explicitly political and utopian philosophy inform EAP, a field implicated in promoting the needs of industry for efficient workers and educational institutions for compliant students? It is precisely because EAP is driven by a pragmatic ideology that it calls out for a more ethical and critical response to academic and workplace requirements. Freire's utopian vision of a society in which teachers and students interrogate the dominant lies (e.g., the rise of English was natural and inevitable) and challenge the limit-situations they face in their daily encounters with injustice provides a needed critical alternative. Even Freire's language of possibility and transformation, his unashamed use of *dream* and *utopia*, offers a stimulating departure from the language of pragmatism in the EAP literature, provoking a desire to interrogate the status quo. However, this perspective is not achieved by critical teachers imposing their vision or political agenda on students as some critics have charged (Santos, in press), but, instead, through a dialogic process, situated in local concerns.

Situatedness and Dialogue

As I discuss in earlier chapters, the greatest strength of EAP is its responsiveness to students' reasons for studying English. It analyzes their purposes for enrolling in a language course and offers instruction focused on those aims. Yet, because needs analysis in EAP is not critical, it is usually little more than an accounting of academic requirements; and, because the instruction is not dialogic, the traditional EAP teacher is mainly a conduit for efficient inculcation of those requirements rather than an activist who could invite students to question them. The monologic nature of EAP is best revealed in the absence of students' voices in the literature. Their reactions to assignments, classes, and texts have, for the most part, not been reported. Exceptions are studies carried out by Fox (1994), Leki (1995, 1999), Leki and Carson (1997), Prior (1995, 1998), Smoke (1994), Spack (1997), and Zamel (1995), who have called for greater attention to student feedback to inform practice.

In their research, students' varied responses to assignments and course activities are documented and examined. Their recommendations for research and instruction take into account students' responses, including those that challenge requirements and change assignment guidelines. However, with few exceptions, such as these authors, EAP's focus on methods and materials, has excluded students' possible participation in curricular and pedagogical decision-making. Perhaps because students are rarely consulted about these issues in academic courses, EAP follows traditional academic procedures, taking its cues from institutional requirements rather than student feedback. Therefore, although EAP is situated in local conditions, an important corrective to English language teaching for vague and unexamined purposes, it is not viewed as a vehicle for questioning or improving those conditions.

Situatedness, in Freirean terms, rejects the notion, embraced by traditional EAP, that teachers should accept and perpetuate externally imposed requirements of the local context. Rather, situatedness means grounding teaching in students' "thematic universe," (Freire, 1970, p. 77), their questions about life in and out of the classroom, often provoked by limit-situations. Education that ignores the condition of students' lives and simply focuses on transferring knowledge denies students their humanity. It refuses the challenge of engaging in a teaching/learning process, called *dialogue*, in which both teacher and student have opportunities to become more fully human. Critical pedagogy is a dialogue about emergent themes that leads to greater understanding of their contradictions and their historical context, and formulation of ways to respond to them.

Dialogic teaching based on limit-situations students face, however, does not preclude attention to external demands and requirements. That is, critical pedagogy should not be misperceived as student-centered, humanistic teaching aiming to raise self-esteem but ignoring the world outside the classroom (Aronowitz, 1998). In rejecting monologic knowledge transfer, critical pedagogy does not leave out the content requirements made on students in their courses or in the workplace. Rather, it treats those demands critically (Benesch, 1999b). Therefore, proposing articulation between Freirean pedagogy and EAP does not mean ignoring academic assignments and activities, nor does it call for basing EAP curricula entirely on themes suggested by students. Rather, a pedagogy of critical EAP must make academic requirements an integral part of its curriculum. In fact, they are, at times, EAP's limit-situation and therefore must be faced with hope and through dialogue with students about how to treat them. Critical EAP allows ESL teachers and students to examine externally imposed demands and negotiate their responses to them, by addressing the following questions: Who formulated these requirements and why? Should they be fulfilled? Should they be modified? What are the consequences of trying to change current conditions? What is gained by obeying, and what is lost? These questions take the limit-situation into account but do not assume that it is immutable. Freire would argue that not engaging students in a dialogue about these questions is unethical because it offers them only one possibility: compliance. Critical EAP offers alternatives to unquestioning obedience, assuming that students have the right to interrogate the demands they face.

The examples of critical EAP in the second half of this book show that the students I teach sometimes perceive academic requirements as unreasonable or ill-conceived, although they do not often articulate their concerns in a clear or organized way. Instead, they engage in a variety of resisting behaviors, including complaints, not doing homework, and arriving late to class, perhaps indicating alienation from academic culture. My role as a critical EAP teacher is to highlight these behaviors as part of students' thematic universe by bringing them into the curriculum for scrutiny. Their role as EAP students and their choices of how to relate to the content course become themes of the EAP class. Then students see themselves as subjects of their learning, with choices about how to respond to limit-situations, rather than objects of lecture and textbook material. They can then choose how to engage with each other, with course material, and with content faculty in a considered manner. The goal is not to make them into well-behaved students happily fulfilling demands but, instead, to view them as members of a community who are aware of various possibilities and who decide which ones to carry out. This is not to say that students are naively unaware of various ways they might respond to a limit-situation but, rather, that critical EAP can draw out individual responses aiming toward collective ones. It moves from individual reactions to a more organized community response. Freire's conceptions of hope and dialogue influence classroom discussions about ways to respond to limit-situations. Foucault's theory of power relations also guides these discussions in ways I examine next.

FOUCAULT: POWER RELATIONS

The promotion of EAP as "service English" (Swales, 1989, p. 79), accepts the positioning of EAP teachers as lower-status members of the academic hierarchy who must win the approval of higher-status content faculty, constructed as "experts" (Johns, 1990b, p. 31). EAP students in this equation are novices or initiates who "must surrender their own language and modes of thought to the requirements of the target community" (p. 33). They must accommodate themselves to the requirements of those communities in order to eventually be accepted by current members, content faculty, who are revered as the arbiters of expertise. Due to the hierarchical nature of these constructions, relationships between teachers and students as well as those between EAP teachers and other members of the academy can be analyzed in terms of power. Foucault's concepts of power offer a lens for understanding traditional EAP's assumption that students are powerless outsiders vis-à-vis academic institutions, although the literature does not explicitly discuss power relations. Instead it reduces students, for the most part, to passive recipients of content and neophytes who strive to gain access to academic discourse communities, accommodating themselves to the language, genres, and activities observed. Foucault's theories also allow for a different type of conceptualization of EAP students as members whose more complicated responses to the status quo, including resistance, can be considered.

Foucault views power not as something that dominant members of society have over subordinate members but, rather, in terms of the relationship between power and resistance. Power and resistance coexist: "there are no relations of power without resistances" (Foucault, 1980, p. 148). Also, according to Foucault, power is "always already there" (Foucault, 1980, p. 141); one can never be outside its domain. In contemporary life, power is not a thing possessed by some at the expense of others but, rather a function of "the strategies, the networks, the mechanisms, all those techniques by which a decision is accepted and by which that decision could not but be taken in the way it was" (Foucault, 1988, p. 104). Studying power, then, is not a matter of identifying heads of state or administrators but, rather, of asking questions about how and why decisions are made: "Who makes decisions for me? Who is preventing me from doing this and telling me to do that? Who is programming my movements and activities? Who is forcing me to live in a particular place when I work in another? How are these decisions on which my life is completely articulated taken?" (Foucault, 1988, p. 103). Though Foucault begins these questions with "who," he is more interested in "how" and "why," the mechanisms of power, how it works strategically. These are the central questions of contemporary life, according to Foucault.

Foucault's (1977) studies of power focus on the body as a site of control. He was interested in ways institutions regulate the body, like the military, schools, hospitals, and prisons. His analyses of "political anatomy" (p. 138) attend to how the movements of soldiers, students, patients, and inmates are controlled through the partitioning of time and space, and how they respond to that control. Spatial partitioning might be examined by studying architecture to observe ways bodies are compelled to move and position themselves due to the way space has been organized. The partitioning of time might be studied by observing ways workers' or students' days are carved up and the resultant regulation of activities and experience. For example, in U.S. secondary schools, the division of a day into numerous time periods, often demarcated by the ringing of a bell, regulates both the quantity and quality of students' encounters with their teachers and course materials. In addition, seating arrangements in classrooms permit certain types of interactions between teachers and students while restricting others. This type of attention to details of time and space management in institutions was one of Foucault's (1980) methods for analyzing "the mechanisms of power that function outside the State apparatuses" at a "minute and everyday level" (p. 60).

Although Foucault (1977, 1980) attends to the regulation of bodies in time and space, he also theorizes resistance as the counterpart to power, thereby taking human agency into account. That is, rather than viewing power as deterministic and all-encompassing, Foucault (1980) relates power and resistance, revealing openings for unanticipated human responses and actions. Humans can, thus, be theorized as subjects actively engaged in the mechanisms of power rather than objects of its control. Yet, resistance does not rule out human susceptibility to regulation, and even self-regulation, when restrictions have been internalized and no longer need to be externally enforced.

An example of the interplay between regulation and resistance in the ELT literature is Pennycook's (1994) Foucauldian analysis of the global spread of English. Although acknowledging Phillipson's (1992) research on the concerted efforts by the United Kingdom and the United States to enforce the use of English around the world, Pennycook objects to the one-sided notion of the dominance of English as exclusively colonizing. This version of events accepts the spread of English "as a priori imperialistic, hegemonic, or linguicist" (p. 69), thereby constructing L2 speakers as the colonized, unengaged in "struggle, resistance, change, human agency or difference" (p. 69). By portraying L2 speakers as those who were forced to abandon their native languages and adopt English language unwittingly, this version leaves out the possibility that English is a site of struggle and resistance for learners who might benefit from appropriating the language for various unanticipated purposes.

Foucault's theory of power offers a framework for studying the dynamics of power and resistance in EAP, in its literature, methods and materials, and the institutions where it is carried out. Analyzing power helps EAP professionals imagine alternatives to the one-dimensional conceptualization of EAP as a service to higher-status disciplines, whose job is to prepare students to accept their circumscribed roles as consumers of information and acquiescent workers. When mechanisms of power are a focus of research, as they were for Foucault (1977), traditionally constructed roles no longer seem natural or inevitable but, rather, the result of institutional arrangements. Viewed as historical decisions, rather than natural ones, current divisions of space and time do not seem immutable but, instead, open to questioning.

Studying the procedures of power raises a different set of questions from those usually posed in EAP, questions affecting needs analysis and curriculum development in novel ways. For example, having observed that a psychology professor's desk sat on a platform raised above the students' desks, arranged in long rows, and that their desks were bolted to the floor, I considered this arrangement in terms of power and resistance (Benesch, 1999a). How did the architect's decision to set up the classroom in this way affect dynamics between the teacher and students? What restrictions did it present? What possibilities did it permit? These questions were echoed in EAP students' complaints to me about the psychology class, particularly the lack of time allowed for discussion between students, such as might happen in small groups. Their concerns led to consideration of how much the architecture contributed to the monologic nature of teacher talk in that class and what possibilities existed for dialogue. (In chap. 7, I discuss students' resistance, in Foucauldian terms, to the nonstop lecturing they encountered and their written proposals for more dialogic teaching.)

When observing the dynamics of power and resistance in various EAP settings, I noticed, as mentioned earlier, that students did not simply comply with the behavioral and procedural requests made by their teachers. Instead, they complained, arrived late to class, allow their attention to wander, and put off assignments. These behaviors are often dismissed in educational settings as simple lack of cooperation or petulant responses to the rigors of academic life. Students are usually exhorted to meet the challenges of the regulations and requirements they face by accommodating themselves to current conditions, which are presented as non-negotiable. Instead, I chose to interpret students' observable behaviors, in a Foucauldian framework, as students' methods for resisting institutional and professorial power. Rather than ignoring students' complaints or advising them to stop complaining and get back to work, I examined their feedback as "pedagogical moments" (Lewis, 1992, p. 169), asking the class to discuss their expectations and disappointments and to formulate proposals for alternatives to the status quo. By understanding their own oppositional behavior as resistance, rather than as acting out, the students were able to reflect collectively on their options within the constraints of the psychology classroom's political anatomy.

During discussions with students about power and resistance, I have found it useful to encourage them to consider their resistance in the wider context of public higher education in New York state, including budget cuts, exclusionary admittance policies, and increased testing, as well as the narrower context of classroom dynamics, assignments, and grades. For example, in the EAP writing course linked to a 450-student psychology lecture course, discussed in chapter 3, students' questions about the size of the lecture class offered an opportunity to discuss the defunding of public higher education leading to larger class size along with termination of discussion sections. These exchanges about budget reductions led to actions, such as letter-writing and participating in university-wide demonstrations, as well as activities to bring about greater interaction between the psychology professor and the EAP students, such as his visit to the class and students' written questions to him (Benesch, 1996).

Without an explicit reckoning of power relations, EAP offers itself only one choice: yielding to the circumscribed institutional role of promoting knowledge transfer while downplaying critical thought. Conceptualizing critical EAP as a dialogic process, driven by hope, taking place within particular institutions, offers alternatives to that narrow, technical role.

FEMINIST PEDAGOGY

Feminist writers (Gore, 1992; Luke, 1992; Weiler, 1994) offer proposals for complicating and refining critical pedagogy, bringing in issues overlooked or trivialized by male writers. While endorsing the goals of social justice and equality in education, these women call for greater situatedness in accounts of critical pedagogy to take students' and teachers' subjectivities and histories into account. They claim that Freire and others, by relying on Marxist and neo-Marxist class-based constructions of concepts, such as *oppression* and *liberation*, have minimized the impact of race, gender, ethnicity, and other subject positions. Greater attention to multiple identities in critical pedagogy is one of their central concerns.

Weiler (1994), for example, pays tribute to Freire's contributions to educational theory and highlights the commonalities between Freirean and feminist pedagogy: "a strong commitment to social justice and a vision of a better world, of the potential for liberation" (p. 13). Yet, she interrogates aspects of his work, in the spirit of offering a "critical feminist re-reading of Freire" (p. 16) whose purpose is to enrich the pedagogy. Two areas Weiler (1994) seeks to complicate are Freire's tendency to universalize experience, knowledge, and truth and his optimistic portrait of teacher authority as dialogic and benign. In addressing the first area of concern, Weiler elaborates a perspective ignored in Freire's theory, what she calls a "feminist pedagogy of difference" (p. 12), that is, attention to students' and teachers' multiple identities and ways they overlap and contradict each other. Weiler points out that Freire (1970), particularly in *Pedagogy of the Oppressed,* assumes a universal experience of oppression, overlooking the varying subject positions of those who might be oppressed and how positionality influences oppression. According to Weiler, Freire dichotomizes oppression, allowing for only two possibilities: oppressor or oppressed. This formulation leaves out what Weiler calls "the specificity of peoples' lives," including ways that they can be oppressed in one situation and privileged in another. Vandrick's (1995) discussion of privileged L2 students enrolled in U.S. universities is an example of this type of overlapping. She points out that these students' elite status positions them as "privileged insiders" by virtue of their elevated social class and can be an area of struggle with their lower-status, middle-class teachers. Yet, the students' identity as "oppressed outsiders" (p. 375), by virtue of their foreign student status, further complicates their identity, creating a contradiction not captured by a monolithic conceptualization of oppression.

Weiler's second area of concern is the question of authority in relationships between teachers and students. She argues that Freire constructs the relationship too optimistically, as a joint project of challenging oppression through a mutually beneficial dialogue. Left out of that description are possible struggles in these relationships due to differences of race, class, age, and gender. Not only may teachers and students have differing goals for critical work due to varying subject positions, but constructions of authority may differ according to the teacher's gender. That is, male and female teachers may have different agendas when it comes to dealing with the authority granted them by the institutions in which they teach. Agreeing with Freire that the institutional authority granted teachers necessitates a vigilance about becoming authoritarian, Weiler explains that for women teachers there is another issue men may not confront, one not taken up by Freire: "the need for women to *claim* authority in a society that denies it to them" (p. 24). That is, having finally been granted a degree of authority in institutions, women may need to assert their authority, both to take ownership of that position, after a long history of being denied, and to model women's authority for both female and male students. So, feminist teachers face the contradiction of promoting democracy in the classroom and maintaining their hard-earned positions of authority in a hierarchical institution.[5] This complication, along with the complexities of varying subject positions in the classroom, must be accounted for in critical feminist teaching, according to Weiler.

Luke (1992) also takes up critical pedagogy's under theorization of gender and subjectivity, opposing its calls for "generalized emancipation from generalized social oppression" (p. 45). She points to the frequent reliance in the critical pedagogy literature on universalist notions of democracy and citizenship, based on the writings of Greek philosophers. These scholars, Luke notes, were interested exclusively in the rights of men as members of society who were considered worthy of public roles and citizenship.

Women were denied places in public life and relegated to the private sphere of domestic life and child-rearing. To evoke democracy and citizenship without problematizing its dualism of public/private life and mental/manual labor is to perpetuate the exclusion of women from the

---

[5]The issue of a feminist teacher's authority is explored in chapter 5 where I discuss anorexia as a topic of study in an EAP writing class, a response to the masculinist subject matter of the psychology lecture class to which it was linked.

public sphere of politics and scholarship, according to Luke (1992). That is, "the patriarchal ideal of equality" (p. 32) must be interrogated. Otherwise, women remain marginalized not only in public life but also in their roles in private life as caretakers. Critical pedagogy must therefore do more than promote dialogic teaching if it is to move beyond its "monogendered class dynamic of historical materialism" (p. 30). Above all, it must recognize that the traditional masculinist bias of educational institutions cannot be dismantled simply by "encouraging critical classroom dialogue and legitimating personal voice *within* the extant structure of schooling." Luke thus cautions against claiming for critical pedagogy more than it can achieve within the serious limitations presented by the academic institutions in which it is often carried out. To address these difficulties, she calls for a focus in feminist pedagogy on "local sites and knowledges" (p. 47), grounded in "a foundation of difference" (p. 48).[6]

Gore (1992) also is leery of the often-grand claims made by male critical pedagogues about the emancipatory possibilities of critical teaching. The focus of her critique is the language of empowerment found in some critical pedagogy publications where, she claims, power is conceptualized as property that can be conferred by someone to another who is then empowered. Gore problematizes this "overly optimistic" (p. 57) view of empowerment, pointing out that teachers are limited by the institutions in which they teach, a similar argument to one made by Luke (1992), and that power is not a commodity that can be passed from a powerful person to a less powerful one who then becomes empowered. To complicate questions of power, Gore turns to Foucauldian notions of power as "exercised" rather than exchanged, claiming: "empowerment cannot mean the giving of power" (p. 59). Instead, teachers can exercise power "in an attempt (that might not be successful) to help others exercise power" (p. 59). That is, teachers can engage in purposeful activities intended to help students exercise power, although the outcomes are not predictable.

To avoid sweeping claims about empowerment and to study how power is exercised in particular classrooms, Gore proposes examining "the microdynamics of the operation of power as it is exercised in particular sites" (p. 59), a Foucauldian formulation. This recommendation echoes ones made by Weiler (1991) and Luke (1992) about the need for greater specificity and contextualization in reports on critical pedagogy. All three writers caution about the need for greater humility to avoid exaggerated

---

[6]Luke's (1992) critique of the masculinist assumptions of critical pedagogy remains abstract. For examples of a critical classroom balancing students' public and private lives, readers might consult Morgan (1998), who presents a well-theorized series of lessons triggered by his mostly female students' private concerns about the depletion of the ozone layer and the possible impact on their children's future. Building from their private fears, Morgan's class moved onto reading about this topic. The lessons included critical discourse analyses of various newspaper articles.

claims about the positive outcomes of critical pedagogy. In place of inflated declarations about how well the pedagogy achieves its empowerment goals, they argue for healthy skepticism and self-criticism both in theorizing critical pedagogy and in reporting from the classroom. This does not mean abandoning political and ethical aspirations but, rather, taking societal and institutional limitations into account along with greater attention to multiple identities being negotiating in a single classroom with a particular group of students.

FREIRE, FOUCAULT, AND FEMINIST CRITICS: INFLUENCES ON CRITICAL EAP

My proposals for critical EAP, and classroom experiments where I have tried to carry it out, are influenced by the theorists just discussed. Due to EAP's unquestioned pragmatism, I have sought ways to bring a critical perspective to EAP, highlighting political and ethical dimensions not usually discussed in the literature. The greatest influence has been Freire's theory of hope, a response to EAP's pragmatic bias. Guided by hope, critical EAP refuses the assumption that prevailing conditions are fixed and that students must unconditionally accept requirements if they are to succeed in academic life and in the larger society. The possibility of altering conditions is reflected in a spirit of optimism in critical EAP classes, as I show in the following chapters. Moments when students resist institutional power are seen as opportunities to problematize power by discussing classroom architecture, the ratio of teacher to student talk, assignments, testing, and evaluation. The experimental nature of hopeful dialogue contributes to an atmosphere of excitement and unpredictability.

Yet, critical EAP exists within the constraints of academic institutions and is therefore limited in what it can achieve in the way of greater gender, racial, ethnic, and class equity, a point made by feminist critics of critical pedagogy's grand theorizing. Awareness of these limitations has also informed my practice. I am simultaneously utopian and grounded in historical inequities that will not be easily overcome, especially in the limited time frame of a semester-long course. Critical EAP does not claim to empower nor does it renounce critical teaching as naive and unrealistic about the obstacles it faces. Rather, it meets the numerous limit-situations academic settings present, not knowing what the final outcome will be. It makes limit-acts possible and then studies what happens as they are enacted, attending to the exercise of power within classroom settings rather than anticipating particular results.

A way to face the complexity of evaluating the success of a limit-act is to focus not on outcomes but, instead, on the microdynamics of power in particular settings, as Gore, following Foucault, proposes. Critical EAP teachers observe ways students exercise and resist power, help students translate their resistance into action, suggest ways to refine their actions, and record the activities and discussions in their work as teacher/researchers. They do all this mindful of the relationship between flexibility and inflexibility in the institutions where they work. This relationship can be explored using both needs analysis to identify requirements and rights analysis to discover possible areas of change, as I explain next.

NEEDS ANALYSIS AND RIGHTS ANALYSIS: RELATING TRADITIONAL AND CRITICAL EAP

Needs analysis takes the world outside the ESL classroom into account, going beyond literature and grammar teaching to prepare students for their future academic experiences. Through faculty surveys, examination of academic writing assignments, analysis of textbooks, observation of classes, and interviews with students, needs analysis offers detailed information about the linguistic and cognitive challenges students face in academic settings. These data can then be used to develop EAP syllabi and instruction appropriate for particular contexts. Like traditional EAP, critical EAP relies on needs analysis to guide activities and assignments, helping students perform well in their academic classes. Examples of linked EAP/content courses in the following chapters show how students went over lecture notes, made sense of textbook material, studied for tests, and collaborated on writing assignments in the EAP class.

Yet, critical EAP goes beyond pragmatic instrumentalism and a limited notion of student success as fulfilling content class requirements. In addition to preparing students for future and concurrent academic assignments, a worthy but insufficient goal, it keeps open the possibility that students might view these assignments as unreasonable, poorly conceptualized, unclear, and so on. Critical EAP helps students articulate and formalize their resistance, to participate more democratically as members of an academic community and in the larger society. *Rights analysis* is a way to conceptualize EAP teaching as more than initiating students unquestioningly into academic discourse communities.

The choice of *rights* as a descriptor is a way to counterpose *needs* with a more explicitly political term, one that underscores power relations in academic settings. *Needs* is a psychological term suggesting that students require or want what the institution mandates. It conflates the private world of desire and the public world of requirements, rules, and regulations. It implies that students will be fulfilled if they follow the rules. In addition, *needs* has a biological connotation, as in basic human needs, such as food, water, and shelter. By conflating learner needs and institutional requirements, needs analysis naturalizes what is socially constructed, making externally imposed rules seem not just normal but also immutable. That is, if students need what institutions offer, there is no apparent conflict. Needs, in this formulation, are not negotiated because they are assumed to be beneficial to students. Discussions of power and opposition are precluded when needs are posited as the centerpiece of EAP.

Rights in critical EAP, on the other hand, highlight academic life as contested, with various players exercising power for different ends. Rights, unlike needs, are political and negotiable. They are a way to conceptualize more democratic participation for all members of an academic community. Rather than viewing students as initiates who must earn their place by adopting the discourse of faculty-experts, as traditional EAP has done, rights analysis assumes students are already members by virtue of paying tuition and taking classes. The degree of participation and influence they can claim for themselves depends on acknowledging learner rights.

Rights, however, are not a set of pre-existing demands but a conceptual framework for questions about power and resistance, such as: What are the explicit and implicit regulations in a particular setting? How do students respond to these regulations? How are decisions about permitted and unpermitted behaviors made? Rights analysis does not assume that students are entitled to certain rights or that they should engage in particular types of activities to claim rights but that the possibility for engagement exists. Rather, it assumes that each academic situation offers its own opportunities for negotiation, depending on local conditions and on the current political climate both inside and outside the educational institution.

Nor are rights in critical EAP seen as artifacts of the Greek model of democratic citizenship, an individualistic notion of male participation and power (Luke, 1992). This model, as Diamond and Quinby (1988) and Luke (1992) demonstrate, relies on a competitive ideal of autonomous beings claiming power for themselves at the expense of others. Because women were excluded from Greek citizenship, the model is inappropriate and anachronistic "without an acknowledgment of [its] deeply embedded masculinist standpoint" (Luke, 1992, p. 33). In place of an individualistic notion of democratic rights, Diamond and Quinby (1988) propose a feminist alternative of "cooperation, community, and communion" (p. 204) along with "connectedness and sharing of responsibilities" in striving for social justice (p. 203). For her part, Luke (1992) calls for accepting "[u]ndecidability, partiality, and contradictory standpoints" rather than claiming to know in advance others' "end points of liberation" (p. 48). That means that rights are contingent, depending on the local context and histories of the participants in a particular course. They emerge from discussions of possible collective responses to local conditions. Critical EAP teachers do not know what might emerge but are prepared to help students enact their reactions in a thoughtful, cooperative, and communitarian fashion. There are examples in the following chapters of students organizing themselves, with my encouragement, to improve conditions for the whole class. The examples demonstrate rights as collective rather than individual.

Critical EAP incorporates needs and rights analysis to take into account both requirements and resistance. Needs analysis is used to study the linguistic and cognitive challenges EAP students face, yet the findings are interrogated rather than unconditionally accepted. Needs analysis grounds EAP in the practical realities of academic assignments, but it overlooks other realities, such as inequities in and out of academic situations. By offering rights analysis as a critical alternative to needs analysis, critical EAP attends to possibilities of more informed democratic participation in academic institutions, in the workplace, and in daily life. It goes beyond an individualistic notion of rights, in hopes of encouraging habits of social cooperation to build healthy, participatory communities. In Part II of this book, the discussions of classroom experiments in which students worked on common goals illustrate this type of community-building.

REFLEXIVITY: PROBLEMATIZING
CRITICAL THEORY AND PRACTICE

Common to all the influences on critical EAP is an assumption that critical teaching ought to be reflexive. That is, to avoid dogmatism and inflated claims about how well it "works," advocates of critical and feminist pedagogies have called for humility and circumspection in their practice and theory. Gore (1992), for example, calls for greater exercise of "humility, skepticism and self-criticism" (p. 68) among critical and feminist teachers. Luke (1992) promotes "serious skepticism" and "critical attention" to counter grand declarations of emancipation and liberation (p. 49). Freire (1998b) is concerned with "critical reflection on practice" (p. 43) to strengthen the relationship between theory and practice. Not only must teachers reflect on their practice as part of their "on-going education," but they must strive to concretize theory so that it can be "clearly identified with practice" (p. 44).

In his introduction to a *TESOL Quarterly* special-topic issue on critical approaches, Pennycook (1999) posits reflexivity as a central concern of critical theory and pedagogy: "self-criticism is a crucial element of critical work" (p. 345). Like Gore (1992) and Luke (1992), he believes critical approaches should incorporate "constant skepticism" and "constant questioning about the types of knowledge, theory, practice, or praxis they operate with" (p. 345). And similar to Gore's and Luke's recommendations for humility, Pennycook urges candor about the limits of what can be known through critical research and practice. This includes problematizing not only research results but also the way one's own research is reported, a feature of the classroom research reports in the following chapters. Reflecting on methodology and results is one of the main principles of critical research, according to Peirce (1995). It is based on a rejection of positivism's claim of objectivity and on support for the assumption that "the researcher plays a constitutive role in determining the progress of the research project" (p. 570).

Recognition of the importance of self-reflection has also made its way in to the ESP literature, in Master's (1998) interrogation of the role of ESP in perpetuating the global domination of English, an issue not previously taken up by mainstream ESP specialists. Master wonders whether the good ESP has done in helping students gain access to greater job opportunities outweighs the harm it has done in promoting the interests of those already in power, thus maintaining traditional power imbalances. By posing this type of question, Master demonstrates ESP's willingness to question itself, what he calls "self-reflective restraint" (p. 725). Language teachers, he believes, should "remain vigilant in regard to all voices, including their own" (p. 724). One way in which ESP can be more vigilant, he says, is to be alert to the possibility that its practice stifles dissent. It can do this by moving from a narrow focus on the academic and workplace discourse toward more comprehensive teaching of English for both specific and general purposes. Master (1998) supports proposals for critical approaches in ESP, believing that the field should orient itself toward distinguishing learner and institutional needs and toward a focus on "reciprocity, not dominance" (p. 724).

SUMMARY

Freire, Foucault, and feminist writers, such as Weiler, Luke, and Gore share an interest in questioning the status quo to probe beyond conventional explanations of why things are the way they are. All are concerned with power relations and with social justice, making their research and practice critical.

Critical EAP assumes that current conditions should be interrogated in the interests of greater equity and democratic participation in and out of educational institutions. It encourages students to assess their options in particular situations rather than assuming they must fulfill expectations. After considering options, they may choose to carry out demands or challenge them. Assessing choices, and their consequences, is a political and ethical process, promoting the formation of community to achieve articulated goals. The examples in the following chapters concretize the theory laid out in this chapter, to clarify its connection to practice.

PART II:

PRACTICE

Chapter 5

Topic Choice in Critical EAP: Revisiting Anorexia

The call for greater reflexivity in both EAP and critical pedagogy, discussed in chapter 4, is answered in this chapter, a re-examination of anorexia as a teacher-selected topic in an EAP curriculum I developed (Benesch, 1998). The EAP course was linked to a psychology lecture course whose curriculum, an introductory survey for undergraduates, focused solely on the contributions of male psychologists and overlooked issues of particular concern to women. I was the EAP teacher and chose to balance the psychology curriculum for gender by devoting 3 weeks of the EAP curriculum to anorexia. Since the publication of the original essay, "Anorexia: A Feminist EAP Curriculum," questions have been raised about that topic choice (Santos, 1998, in press). In this chapter, I examine those questions in the context of a broader concern in the L2 composition literature that teaching students to think critically is a form of social indoctrination that imposes the teacher's social agenda (Atkinson, 1997, 1999; Atkinson & Ramanathan, 1995; Ramanathan & Kaplan, 1996a, 1996b, Santos, 1998, in press). My aim is, in part, to respond to the arguments related to indoctrination. Yet, in the name of reflexivity, I also consider ways I might have dealt with the masculinist curriculum of the linked psychology class besides assigning anorexia as a topic of study, especially ways that might have promoted greater dialogue about the psychology and EAP syllabi.

To set the context, I begin by describing the linked psychology/EAP writing course and by reviewing the rationale for choosing the topic of anorexia. Next, I discuss Santos' (in press) critique of that choice as well as related literature opposing the teaching of critical thinking to non-native speaking students in U.S. universities. Then, I review the choice of anorexia in light of the relationship between teacher imposition and student resistance. Finally, I consider alternatives to choosing anorexia in the context in which that choice was made, including student-selection of topics and whole-class problematizing of the psychology and EAP curricula.

INSTRUCTIONAL CONTEXT

The setting of the linked EAP/psychology course was an urban college where I was a visiting associate professor during the 1994–95 academic year. I taught ESL writing classes, including one linked EAP writing/psychology survey course each semester. The introductory psychology course was a biweekly lecture with 400 to 500 students taught by two members of the psychology department who alternated lecturing on the syllabus topics: history of psychology; research methods, brain/behavior; perception; consciousness; development; learning; motivation and emotion; memory; personality; abnormal behavior; treatment; social psychology; and industrial psychology. Although the professors were skilled and compelling lecturers, they could not offer more than a superficial treatment of the topics nor could they engage students in extensive discussion, given the size of the syllabus and the class. The two psychology teachers were painfully aware of the limitations of a survey course whose discussion sections had been cut due to a reduced university budget. Both hoped the linked EAP classes would offer more engaged and personal experiences for the students. They also regretted having to grade students solely on the basis of scores received on three multiple-choice exams rather than on multiple measures. The lack of personal contact with students was an additional source of frustration to them.

The EAP students (15 in the fall semester and 10 in the spring semester) had failed the university's Writing Assessment Test (WAT) and had subsequently been assigned to the intermediate level of the English department's ESL writing courses, paired with psychology. The department's goals for the EAP writing course were to link language and content learning and prepare students to retake the WAT. I added a third goal: balancing the curriculum for gender. This was due to a notable lack of attention in the psychology syllabus to women's psychology and women psychologists, aside from Anna Freud, who was mentioned only in the context of her psychoanalysis of Erik Erikson, to whom two lectures were devoted. An area of study I thought would redress the exclusion of women was anorexia, a topic discussed on one page of the psychology textbook in the chapter on "Motivation and Emotion" and mentioned in one lecture, as a definition to be memorized for an upcoming test. That is, it was part of the psychology curriculum, yet not presented in any depth, as is the case with most topics in a survey course.

I introduced the topic by assigning Levenkron's (1978) *The Best Little Girl in the World*, a fictional case study of an upper middle-class anorexic adolescent girl living in Manhattan. The author, a psychologist who treats anorectics, offers an accessible account of the girl's struggle, attributed mainly to birth order and family dynamics. The main character is the youngest of three children whose parents ignore her, while paying attention to the successful first-born son and the overtly maladjusted second-born daughter. The protagonist's anorexia is attributed to a striving for perfection, self-denial, and self-control as ways to gain adult approval and attention. A major drawback of the novel is that it offers little insight into anorexia as a social condition, instead portraying it as the private struggle of a lonely and confused young woman. Still, it does suggest that self-starvation is a way for young women to reduce the space they take up rather than asserting their place and space in society (Bartky, 1988), an issue I wanted the students to consider.

Students took double-entry notes on *The Best Little Girl in the World*, writing quotes from the text on one page and commentary about those quotes on the facing page. They later consulted the notes to write research questions and then to collaboratively develop research areas: psychological causes; environmental causes; outcomes; treatment; image. They then formed research groups, gathered articles, wrote individual research papers, and presented their research in groups to the rest of the class, allowing for sharing of knowledge beyond what they had learned in their individual projects.

CRITIQUE OF CRITICAL EAP
AND CRITICAL THINKING

Santos' (in press) concerns about choosing anorexia revolve around the appropriateness of an EAP teacher choosing a theme for a whole class to write about, especially one Santos characterizes as fulfilling a "social agenda":

> Wouldn't a choice of topics have led to a more desirable diversity of course material, especially if brief oral presentations had accompanied the assignment so students could hear about each others' topics? Even more important, a choice would have allowed students to research and write about something that interested them, not Benesch's social agenda. Her requirement of a specific type of assignment was a throwback to a time in academia when professors typically set writing topics because they wanted uniformity and believed they knew best what students should write on. Current approaches to writing have moved away from that in favor of student choice, and it is ironic that it should be a critical "liberatory" approach to teaching which brings back teacher-imposed topics for the sake of social/political consciousness raising (Santos, in press)

Santos' comments about teacher imposition of a social agenda through the selection of a particular topic can be considered in the larger context of the literature opposing the teaching of critical thinking[7] to non-native speaking students enrolled in composition courses in U.S. universities (Atkinson, 1997, 1999; Atkinson & Ramanathan, 1995; Ramanathan & Kaplan 1996a, 1996b). These authors caution that critical thinking, which they construct as a uniquely Western mode of thought, should not be taught because to do so "impose[s] on all students one way of ordering or making sense of the world" (Ramanathan & Kaplan, 1996b, p. 230). To avoid imposition, they offer alternatives to critical thinking. For example, Ramanathan and Kaplan (1996b) propose teaching academic genres, finding that they are "freer of cultural constraints" (p. 242) than critical thinking. For his part, Atkinson (1998) calls for "cognitive apprenticeship" (p. 89) in which skills demanded by the target situation are modeled by the teacher–expert for the student–apprentices who practice them in small groups until achieving mastery. Cognitive apprenticeship, Atkinson claims, is a "pan-cultural model" (p. 89) of teaching writing that takes into account the "cultural and social-practice nature of all significant learned experience" (p. 87).

Efforts made to find a universal way of teaching apparently neutral skills are based on an assumption that culture can be transcended and imposition avoided. The opponents of teaching critical thinking propose what they believe are culture-free or pan-cultural modes of teaching L2 composition and censure the work of those whose social agendas are explicitly stated. Missing from their stance on critical teachers' imposition of social agenda is a recognition that all forms of teaching are political, including academic genres and cognitive apprenticeship, and that imposition is unavoidable. Also left out is a notion of student agency and resistance balancing teacher authority. That is, according to this literature, students are susceptible to the unquestioning absorption of critical teachers' political agendas, not possibly active participants in dialogic teacher–student relationships. The coexistence of power and resistance in those relationships is not recognized.

The interaction between teacher imposition and student resistance is taken up in the discussion of the EAP class where anorexia was a topic of study. First, however, I compare how process and critical approaches theorize topic choice and then how EAP has traditionally dealt with topic choice.

TOPIC CHOICE IN CRITICAL AND WRITING PROCESS APPROACHES

Examples of critical pedagogy often show how themes emerged through dialogue with students about issues affecting their daily lives (Auerbach &

---

[7]Ramanathan and Kaplan (1996b) describe teaching critical thinking as "(1) developing students' sense of informal logic toward strengthening their reasoning strategies; (2) developing and refining problem-solving skills; (3) developing the ability to look for hidden assumptions and fallacies in arguments" (p. 226). Atkinson (1997) reviews the literature on critical thinking and concludes that is a "social practice" (p. 73) characteristic of U.S. middle-class thinking.

McGrail, 1991; Morgan 1992/3,1998). The guiding principle is that the curriculum is an ongoing negotiation based on the interests, desires, and needs of the students, not a predetermined syllabus imposed by the teacher or institution (Anderson & Irvine, 1993; Wink, 1997). Yet, Freire (1970) and others, including those who practice "problem-posing," challenge the notion that topic choices must always be negotiated in critical classrooms. In fact, they argue against conceptualizing critical curriculum development as a series of steps to follow, what Aronowitz calls the "fetish of method" (Aronowitz, 1993). The emphasis is more on *how* topics are studied, dialogically rather than didactically, than on *who* chooses or *what* is chosen. Freire, for example, does not insist that students select topics but that the classroom be dialogic so that the participants study together to develop greater understanding. The object of study, no matter who proposes it, provides an opportunity for the teacher and student to participate in a rich and challenging dialogue affecting all the participants:

> The object to be known in one place links the two cognitive subjects, leading them to reflect together on the object. Dialogue is the sealing together of the teacher and students in the joint act of knowing and re-knowing the object of study. Then, instead of transferring knowledge *statically*, as a *fixed* possession of the teacher, dialogue demands a dynamic approximation towards the object. (Shor & Freire, 1987, p. 100)

Despite critical pedagogy's flexibility on topic choice, Santos (in press) suggests that my decision to assign anorexia, rather than having students select their own topics, was hypocritical, an oppressive move by a teacher masquerading as "liberatory." The flaw in this analysis is that it conflates "current approaches to writing," presumably process approaches with their preference for student choice of writing topics, and what Santos calls a "critical 'liberatory' approach to teaching," which does not share this insistence, as I demonstrated previously. By not distinguishing the different ideologies of process and critical pedagogies and focusing solely on topic choice, Santos misses important distinctions between them. Berlin's (1988) discussion of expressionistic (process) and social–epistemic (critical) rhetorics provides the missing contrast.

According to Berlin (1988), expressionistic rhetoric, advocated by Elbow (1973, 1981) and Murray (1969), is concerned with helping students find their "unique voice" (Berlin, 1988, p. 486). It resists adherence to the status quo but only insofar as society's hierarchical arrangements suppress individuals' desire to express themselves. The goal of the expressionistic teacher is to free writers so they can transcend these arrangements privately. It is a rhetoric of individualism, a search for the "true self," a personal quest for fulfillment rather than a collective response to injustice and inequality. Methodologically speaking, expressionism focuses on student choice of topic and avoids teacher imposition so as not to interfere in the search for self.

Berlin describes expressionism's response to authoritarianism in society and in the classroom as "each lighting one small candle in order to create a brighter world" (p. 487), perhaps a sly reference to former U.S. president George Bush's "thousand points of light" 1988 campaign slogan, promoting individual volunteerism and liberal do-goodism as a response to social ills rather than a radical rethinking of the social order and organization of the disenfranchised to achieve greater equality.

Social–epistemic rhetoric, on the other hand, focuses on making students aware that they are socially constructed, not autonomous, beings. Identity is not a matter of finding one's "true self" but, rather, of discovering various ways one is constructed according to class, race, gender, ethnicity, age, and so on. The unequal arrangements that "alienate and disempower" (Berlin, 1988, p. 492) are highlighted and students are given opportunities to locate themselves in current social arrangements and decide if they want to support or challenge them.

So, one response to Santos' surprise that a critical teacher would assign a topic rather than inviting students to choose their own, is that critical EAP does not encourage students to find their unique "voice" by mining their private experience for writing topics, as in expressionistic rhetoric. Rather, it creates ways for students to collectively consider their socially constructed identities and the conditions in which they live, offering choices they might not have imagined before participating in a dialogic classroom (Benesch, 1999b; Morgan, 1998).

The ideological distinctions between expressionistic and social–epistemic rhetorics are part of the answer to Santos' critique. As I discuss next, another response is to point out the inconsistency between the expressionistic position that EAP students choose their own topics and the mainstream EAP position that they should not choose.

TOPIC CHOICE IN TRADITIONAL EAP

EAP syllabus design is based on needs analysis and thus adheres to academic requirements. Therefore, traditional EAP's position on topic choice has been that allowing students to make their own selections neglects to prepare them for the authentic academic experience. Horowitz (1986a, 1986b), for example, states that EAP teachers should not let their students choose topics because they "rarely have a free choice of topics in their university writing assignments)(Horowitz, 1986a, p. 143). Encouraging choice, he asserts, would be a disservice to ESL students who must learn to adapt to the teacher-developed syllabi of typical content classes. EAP teachers should therefore prepare students for academic writing by assigning topics rather than permitting student choice: "Teaching students to write intelligently on topics they do not care about seems to be a more useful goal than having them pick topics which interest them" (Horowitz, 1986a, p. 143).

Hutchinson and Waters (1987) take a similar position, believing that a learner-centered approach to ESP, where students choose the subject matter, is untenable because predetermined syllabi are the rule in educational institutions and students must learn to meet target situation expectations.

Santos (in press), although calling into question the teacher-imposed topic of anorexia in my EAP writing class, seems to support the mainstream EAP position of accepting academic requirements as the basis of syllabus design. She advocates teaching academic discourse conventions as the only ethical position, one that would seem to preclude student choice of topics:

> I certainly find nothing ethically disgraceful in helping students accommo-
> date to, or assimilate into, the dominant academic discourse(s), since I regard
> this as essential for academic success; in fact, I would consider it unethical *not*
> to do so.

Given this stance, it appears that Santos' concerns about my imposition of anorexia is not about *choice* per se but about *which choice*. This might explain why she does not express opposition to teacher-assigned topics in content courses, such as the psychology class to which my EAP class was linked, but does oppose the teacher-made choice of anorexia in the EAP class. Nor does she object to other choices I made for the same syllabus, including assigning the popular classic, Axline's (1964) *Dibs in Search of Self*, on the use of play therapy to treat a severely disturbed child. Her silence on these matters can be interpreted as valorizing canonical choices, such as *Dibs* and all the topics on the psychology syllabus, while opposing noncanonical ones, those she interprets as fulfilling the critical teacher's social agenda. That is, content-course syllabi are considered immutable, yet critical EAP's are open to question. The imperative to offer choice in the EAP class is set aside when it comes to bolstering content-course objectives.

Despite Santos' problematic preference for some teacher-imposed topics (e.g., academic discourse conventions) over others (e.g., anorexia), I am not ready to abandon the question about whether EAP teachers, traditional or critical, should assign research/writing topics. Instead, it is worth considering the advantages and disadvantages of teacher and student-selected topics in critical EAP, an issue taken up later in this chapter. For now, I turn to the dialogic relationship between teacher imposition and student resistance, a response to the criticism that students are vulnerable to teachers' social agendas.

TEACHER IMPOSITION
AND STUDENT RESISTANCE

I imposed the topic of anorexia just as my colleagues in the psychology department imposed the topics on their syllabus. In fact, anorexia was part of the official psychology curriculum, yet treated so superficially that students had no chance to understand its significance in their lives. They simply memorized a definition for a test: "Anorexia nervosa: An eating disorder usually striking young women in which symptoms include various degrees of starvation in an attempt to avoid obesity." {Feldman, 1993, p. 350). As was the case with most topics presented in the lecture class, no opportunities to explore the topic were provided.

Yet, as Foucault's theory of power underscores, imposition is not the full story. Students met the teacher-selected topic with a variety of responses: opposition; testimonials; questions; interest; boredom; disgust; compassion; identification; and surprise. The dialogic treatment of the topic encouraged further expression of this range of response. Students did not passively absorb information nor were they brainwashed by my thinking. In fact, it is hard to imagine how I could have made them think as I did about the topic because my own thinking changed as we read the novel, as I listened to the connections students made during class discussions, and as I read their journals and research papers. I began the fall-semester linked course thinking I could balance the psychology curriculum for gender but with a vague notion of what that meant. I saw it as an opportunity to explore an issue reaching in to many aspects of young women's lives but was unsure of what their reactions might be.

The resistance of three male students to studying anorexia was a major focus of "Anorexia: A Feminist EAP Curriculum" (Benesch, 1998). As I explain in that article, one young man in the fall semester, Chen, and two young men in the spring, Sasha and George, opposed the subject matter. Rather than viewing these instances of resistance as a sign of failure, though, I welcomed them as pedagogical or political moments (Lewis, 1992), opportunities for dialogue rather than indications that I should abandon the topic.

Chen complained that *The Best Little Girl in the World* was boring the day the class began discussing the first set of double-entry notes. When I asked him why, he replied that it had nothing to do with him. To get him to test his claim that eating and eating disorders were not issues he needed to consider, I asked if he ever went out with female friends for lunch or dinner. When he answered that he did, I asked what they ordered. "They're all on diets! All they order is diet soda!" he replied. Next, I asked if he thought they needed to diet, and he answered that they could lose a few pounds. This exchange prompted several of the young women in the class to discuss their fear of gaining weight and their inhibitions about eating in front of men because it is "unfeminine behavior." They also examined Chen's declaration that his female friends *could lose a few pounds*, wondering how that motif affected their daily lives. The men were surprised to hear the women's testimonials, explaining that they did not experience similar constraints related to eating and body image. Chen's complaint, then, triggered an important discussion about how the social construction of women might differ from men's in their relationships to food and body image. That discussion was not abstract, but grounded in the concrete realities of their everyday thoughts and activities.

Where Chen complained about the topic only once, George's and Sasha's resistance was more constant, coming through in their double-entry notes and in class discussions. George's response to the novel was that the protagonist was "crazy" and "silly," terms he used throughout the time the class studied anorexia. After one of the final activities, an in-class viewing of a television special on a Canadian treatment facility for anorectics that included graphic shots of emaciated girls, George exclaimed, "They're crazy!" indicating that he had not developed empathy for those afflicted with eating disorders. Given that one purpose of studying psychology is to develop understanding of various disorders and compassion for people whose behavior is unfamiliar or disturbing, I problematized the use of "crazy," to describe hypochondriacs, schizophrenics, and sociopaths, whose disorders had been discussed in the lectures, as well as anorectics. Although George did not participate in the ensuing discussion, other students expressed an understanding of "crazy" as dismissive rather than tolerant.

Like George, Sasha distanced himself from the study of anorexia, explaining in his written responses to the novel that he neither understood the problem nor was interested in trying to understand, a stance he had not taken toward any of the other material presented in either the EAP or psychology classes. One of his journal entries delineates this position:

> I think, think, think and can't get in the inside world of this child. Why did she give up with everything, but not with the starvation? And what is strange, I don't want to know the reason. I'm not interested in the whole topic of anorexia. Maybe I'll be interested in it later, when I'll may be have a daughter, but for now it is very boring for me. I mean, I'm really sorry for her, but all that girl problems are not my style. Sorry for those words, but at least I'm being honest.

My response to this journal entry was private: "Thanks for being honest." To make it a pedagogical moment, I could have sought his permission to write the entry on the board and ask for reactions. It would have been an opportunity to discuss why some topics seem more interesting than others and what Sasha meant by "girl problems are not my style." Two of Sasha's other journal entries might also have been candidates for whole-class inquiry because they raise issues about the male gaze: His impatience with the main character centered on her turning her body into an undesirable object:

> Only skin and bones. I guess no breast—is it looks nice for her? She is really crazy. She doesn't even understand the danger of this condition. . . .

> I think that when the woman is real thin, then she doesn't have anything good in her body. The body has to be shaped in a nice round manner. And the bones

don't make it beautiful. I'd like to see someone who says that sceleton is more cute than, for instance, Marlin Monroe.

[I regret not providing the opportunity to discuss these passages. A study of Sasha's strict specifications for desirability might have led to fruitful discussion of the social construction of female beauty, including the role of the male gaze.]

While "Anorexia: A Feminist EAP Curriculum" (Benesch, 1998) focused, in part, on male opposition, it did not present the more favorable ways male students reacted to the topic. For example, another Russian student in the spring semester, Andrey, had a different kind of response, expressing empathy for the main character and admiration for her stubborn devotion to weight loss: "She is a girl of a lot of internal strength. A type of person who would detest to be seen crying or complaining. Ever since she was born she was used to lack of attention. It made her be on her own and strong-headed." He also showed interest in the topic itself, as indicated in the final journal entry: "The topic of anorexia was the one that I most liked because I didn't know what it was until now, especially in such detailed definitions." And, his final research paper, "Anorexia and Men" includes interesting personal connections between men, food, health, and anorexia:

> I look in the mirror every morning and complain to my self that it looks like I'm growing a stomach and that I need to start exercising and eat just dinner, maybe start smoking again because it will keep me from eating. I never thought there was anything wrong with that up until now.

Inviting the class to discuss the differences in Sasha's and Andrey's responses to the topic, had I gotten their permission to do so, might have produced interesting observations about why one saw it exclusively as a "girl problem" while the other identified with the problem, of body image and control.

Santos (in press) views the resistance of Chen, George, and Sasha as confirmation that I imposed my social agenda on the students. However, as I have suggested, their resistance seems, instead, to demonstrate that they felt entitled to participate in a dialogue rather than absorbing or silently resisting a monologically taught curriculum. Their comfort with opposing my topic choice, in George's and Sasha's cases throughout the time anorexia was studied, was apparent. My role was to maintain a dialogue about the topic and encourage whatever responses emerged. I should add that I welcomed the remarks of all the students, encouraging participation of any kind. The open resistance of a few to studying anorexia was not coupled with or met with antagonism or ill-will. Nor did it reflect in the quality of their work, all of which was handed in on time and completed satisfactorily. In fact, my desire to maintain goodwill in the classroom may have prevented me from pressing issues raised by Sasha in his written responses; I may have inadvertently short-circuited further dialogue on important questions appearing in his journal entries by not encouraging him to go public with them.

Although I have not yet described reactions of any of the young women in the fall or spring EAP classes, their contributions also relate to the question of imposition and resistance. That is, in choosing anorexia, I created openings for expression that are resisted in the academic world: Women theorizing from their experience. In the next section, I explore that issue.

TEACHER IMPOSITION AND RESPONSES
OF FEMALE STUDENTS

My goal in assigning anorexia was to have students engage deeply with one of the many topics introduced in the linked psychology class. And, as previously mentioned, I wanted to balance the psychology curriculum for gender by choosing an issue affecting women more directly than men. Also, I was interested in addressing what I see as a social and public health issue: young women's fear of gaining weight and the dangerous lengths they will go to avoid it. In the original essay (Benesch, 1998), I express concern that my students' responses to the topic and readings were more psychological than social due to the orientation of *Best Little Girl in the World* (Levenkron, 1978) and the popular literature they studied for their research projects. Although I still believe that social models could have balanced the predominant psychological/medical one, I nonetheless think that studying anorexia allowed female students to consider their relationships to food, body image, and self-surveillance. That is, I am claiming that anorexia provided opportunities to connect private concerns and academic study in ways that other topics had not. Although the long-term benefits of that engagement are unknown, responses of some of the women indicate that this topic has great potential for legitimizing the participation and experience of female students in academic life.

One example is a Dominican student, Ana, who expressed doubt about her preparation for the linked classes on the first day the EAP class met. She had attended junior high and high school in the New York City public school system, yet failed all three CUNY Freshman Skills Assessment Tests on entry (reading, writing, and math). She was therefore one of two students in the spring semester enrolled in ESL reading, ESL writing, and remedial math. So, although Ana had been in the United States longer than any of the other students, she felt less entitled to be in college, even in ESL classes, than some of the more recent arrivals from, for example, Russia, Bulgaria, and Argentina, who had passed the reading and math tests but not writing. After the first day of the EAP class, Ana told me she wanted to drop the linked courses, having decided that her classmates, some of whom had read their in-class writing out loud, were more proficient writers of English. I encouraged her not to leave, thinking that the social support of a link would serve her better than a stand-alone ESL writing class. Fortunately, Ana stayed and she improved throughout the semester, failing her first psychology exam but receiving B on the second and third. Even though that increased success can be attributed to a variety of factors, including practice psychology tests in the EAP class and the community provided by the link, studying anorexia seemed to solidify her participation in the class through the accessibility of *Best Little Girl in the World* (Levenkron, 1978) and its clear connection to her life outside of college. This connection is underscored in her written feedback about the EAP class on the final day of the semester:

> The topic of anorexia was the one that I liked most. Now I can analize that I have several friends (girls) with that problem of anorexia. Before I used to make jokes of them thinking that they were crazy because they wanted to be skinnier, but now I understand they have a problem, a psychological problem and that I feel the rights to try to help them.

It is interesting to note that one of Ana's goals for studying psychology, written on the first day of the EAP class was "to know how to advice and help people about any problems they should have and also to help myself about some confusion that I almost all the time have with my live." Examining anorexia was a way for her to fulfill that goal by relating her personal and academic lives.

The most dramatic example of that connection, though, was Julia, an upper middle-class Argentinian student, enrolled in the spring semester, with personal experience as an anorectic. Her lengthy double-entry notes combined testimonials, in which she identified with the main character, with attempts to better understand what she had gone through herself. While reading the novel, she came to realize that some of her anorexic behaviors persisted though she had thought herself "cured":

> What makes me feel scared is that I still have some habits while eating. For ex-ample, if I buy a hamburger, I would break the pieces and put it on the plate, eat some of the burger and leave it like that . . . In fact, I realize this now, after reading this book.

Julia served as the resident expert, generously sharing her knowledge and offering evidence that this disorder was not mythical or abstract. Her struggle to come to terms with her experience, including her research paper on its social causes, allowed other students to see that this issue was not confined to textbooks or novels. It also showed Julia that her private experience was worthy of academic study.

Other women in the class with no direct experience with anorexia, nonetheless, also wanted to understand it deeply. Questions in their double-entry notes probed the causes, wondering about the state of mind of a thin woman who believed she was fat. These students seemed dissatisfied with Levenkron's (1978) explanation that family psychodynamics were the exclusive cause of anorexia and looked for a more complex analysis of the problem, as these excerpts from three different journals show:

> I'm really interested in the mind of Francesca. She had different view on her appearance with the others. Base on the common view, She is so thin that looks terrible. However, in her own mind, she thinks she looks good.

> What I don't understand is that why does she want to be this skinny? And for who does she want to be like that? People usually tend to change themselves because of what other people think, and if people around them are happy with the way they look, then they're happy with it also. I know that people exaggerate when it comes to the way they look, especially body weight, but doesn't she realize that she lost enough weight already since everybody seems to tell her that? What kind of state of mind could she possibly be into?

> I'm still not clear about Francesca's fear of food. Maybe she's afraid to eat because by doing so she will lose the attention she now gets. But is this reason sufficient enough? Can the fear of being ignored again transform into a fear of food?

↗ inclusion of student reaction

(These questions were discussed in peer groups where students shared their double-entry notes and decided which themes to bring to the whole-class discussion. Their research topics were also based on questions from their notes. However, reviewing the data, I now believe that questions about distorted body image and the social causes of anorexia should have been addressed more directly by relying on feminist texts, such as Bordo (1993) and Bartky (1988). At the time, I was concerned that their analyses of women's relationships to food as social phenomena, though apt, were too abstract to contribute to the classroom conversation. Yet, I now think I underestimated my students' ability to read such prose. For example, Bordo's presentation of the contradictions of slenderness might have been a useful tool for getting at students' questions about the possible causes of anorexia and an anorectic's state of mind.)

> Female slenderness, for example, has a wide range of sometimes contradictory meanings in contemporary representations, the imagery of the slender body suggesting powerlessness and contraction of female social space in one context, autonomy and freedom in the next. (Bordo, 1993, p. 26)

This brief yet rich hypothesis might have answered some of the questions about body image, offering a useful tool for discussing the relationship between power and powerlessness in anorexia. Another theoretical tool might have been Bordo's (1993) positing of anorexia and bulimia at the extreme end of a continuum that includes chronic fear of weight gain and compulsive exercising and dieting on the part of women and, increasingly, girls who are "subject to the same sociocultural pressures" (p. 61). The continuum is a compelling image to bridge the gap between the extreme of eating disorders and the more familiar self-surveillance my female students were subject to.

In addition to theoretical interventions such as quotes from Bordo (1993), I now think I should have proposed additional modalities for the research projects to allow consideration of various types of data. For example, students could have combined library work with surveys of fellow students, friends, and family members on body image, eating habits, and other issues they wanted to analyze. The surveys would have offered experience in field research as well as connections between daily and academic life, while answering their questions.

Although improvements could be made to studying anorexia, I believe it was an important way to highlight women's concerns and voices in the EAP class. The psychology curriculum presented academic subject matter as the province of male experts whose ideas were to be memorized not questioned. Students were apprentices; their psychology professors were members of a discourse community that appeared, according to the syllabus, to be the exclusive province of men, such as Watson, Skinner, Freud, Erikson, and so on. Studying anorexia allowed for a variety of voices, including Julia's, whose personal experience emerged as a source of expertise. Even though anorexia was not a student-selected topic, their questions guided its analysis, including Chen's and Sasha's about whether it should be studied in the first place.

Above all, the voices of students trying to understand eating disorders at a deep level of engagement stand out. These are the compelled voices of women and men trying to fathom self-starvation and self-surveillance as a way to understand themselves and their friends. It served particularly to encourage greater participation by women, whose experience is not always valued as a legitimate subject of academic study.

Having described the classes in which anorexia was assigned, I next discuss the merits of student-selected topics, offering an example from a different linked class. My purpose here is to consider the advantages and disadvantages of student choice in critical EAP and to propose a third scenario: whole-class choice of a common topic, as perhaps the most democratic option. This does not mean, though, that I am ruling out teacher-selected topics. Rather, I believe that both teacher and student choice of topics have a place in critical EAP.

STUDENT-SELECTED TOPICS IN CRITICAL EAP

When students choose their own topics, they can focus more closely on an area of interest and, as Santos (in press) points out, they can present their research to the other students, offering diverse subjects to learn about. This was the case in a linked social science/EAP reading class I taught in 1998. Students were instructed to rely on their experience and interest when choosing a research topic from the social science textbook or EAP textbook, a collection of magazine and journal articles on sociology. They selected: dating violence, capital punishment, euthanasia, teenage violence, crime in the United States, domestic violence, food scarcity, racial inequality, and affirmative action. One disadvantage of self-selection was that the variety of topics excluded the possibility of in-depth, whole-class scrutiny of a particular area. Another disadvantage was that students who had less compelling reasons for choosing their topics seemed to pick randomly and were therefore not as engaged as others. That is, offering students a choice of topics does not guarantee that they will be strongly attached to the one they select.

Despite these limitations, certain advantages emerged from self-selection. One is that when students initially shared their topic choices with the rest of the class, some asked for explanations of the choices, leading to productive discussion of unexplored questions and beliefs. For example, after three female students announced separately that they would be studying dating or domestic violence, one male student, Leo, asked what these terms meant and, after they were defined, remarked, "Why are you all studying violence against women? Is it a big problem? Do your boyfriends beat you up?" His questions were met by nervous laughter but then by serious discussion of the issue. The women gave reasons for choosing these topics, including that they wanted to avoid violent dates and marriages and that they had friends who had faced physical abuse from men. Leo was intrigued by their responses and looked forward to hearing the results of their research. In fact, he decided to switch his own topic to "gender inequality" as a way to explore issues the women had raised.

Two other men in the class, Joon and Roger, responded to the choices of domestic and dating violence more defensively. They expressed a belief that female violence against men was a bigger problem than the reverse and decided, on the spot, to study that topic rather than the ones they had originally picked, to confirm their belief. The ensuing discussion led to a clarification: Men hit women, Roger speculated, after being provoked by women, so the beating was justified. Sometimes the provocation was physical, other times verbal, but it was always initiated by the woman. Roger also explained that he wanted to avoid becoming an abuser, but worried that he might not be able to if he found himself provoked. He thought the research would help him come to terms with this dilemma. Indeed, when he encountered convincing statistics about domestic violence by men toward women during his search and found nothing about female violence toward men, he began to reconsider his original position. He admitted to me privately that he thought men tried to justify their beatings by blaming women for provoking them. In the end, he abandoned the topic, switching to racism and poverty. Joon, on the other hand, stayed with the topic of domestic violence but shifted the focus to abuse by men of women, having found no articles on wives who beat their husbands.

This example reveals some advantages of student selection. One is that their choices may inspire other students to confront issues they have not previously considered. Another is that topics teachers may consider too "hot," such as domestic violence, may be more readily accepted when proposed by students. And, finally, teachers cannot always predict issues their students will find compelling. So, although opportunities to collaborate in gathering and presenting material is lost when the class does not work on a common theme, there are clear benefits to student selection.

The most effective way to engage students might be to try a mix of teacher and student choice with whole-class selection of a theme as a third alternative. Each possibility has its benefits:

1. teacher-generated themes allow students to fulfill externally imposed requirements, an essential component of an EAP class whose students are in or will be in content classes where no choice is offered;

2. individual student choice allows for a wider selection of research areas and sharing of findings with others; and

3. whole-class selection of a shared topic requires democratic decision making, an important component of community building in a critical classroom.

Having explored some advantages and disadvantages of student-selected topics, I now turn to other ways I might have responded to the masculinist curriculum of the psychology, ways that might have offered a more participatory experience through negotiation of the EAP curriculum.

ALTERNATIVES TO ANOREXIA

Although I did find positive outcomes of imposing anorexia as a topic of study, in retrospect I can imagine alternatives to that selection based on problematizing syllabi and topics with students so that they can participate more fully in constructing the curriculum. That is, rather than developing the syllabus myself, following needs and rights analyses of the psychology curriculum, I might have engaged students in coconstructing the EAP curriculum as they discovered the demands of the psychology class. Together we would have figured out ways to respond to it.

For example, having noticed that the psychology syllabus excluded the contributions of women, I might have raised this issue with the class to see what their reactions would be. They might have suggested ways to compensate for this exclusion, other than ones I might have imagined on my own.

– put topic on syllabus?
– leave it up to discussion

Or, supposing I had suggested anorexia as a topic of research as a way to incorporate an issue of particular concern to women rather than including it on the syllabus as a fait accompli. The ensuing discussion might have been a fruitful exchange about whether or not the students wanted to study it, one option being that not everyone would.

Finally, as mentioned before, the negative reactions of some of the men to studying anorexia could have been an area of inquiry, focusing on their written responses. Reasons for the lack of interest in this topic might have opened up the question of what gets included in an academic syllabus and what gets left out. Questions about who chooses the areas of study, which books are selected, and why those choices are made could have been addressed.

What these alternatives suggest is that by problematizing their practice, critical EAP teachers can engage students in all aspects of syllabus design, making them aware that curricula are socially constructed by humans with social agendas, not natural or "normal" phenomena.

SUMMARY

At the end of the fall and spring semesters, I asked EAP students to give written feedback about the class, based on the following questions: Which activities did you find most beneficial? Which activities did you find least beneficial? What suggestions do you have to improve the class? Sasha offered the following suggestion: "I'd like to do some library research on some interesting topic, but different from what others do. So, I will be interested in what they say and they'll be interested in what I say." Sasha is expressing a preference for students choosing their own topics so they can research what interests them and share their different findings. I agree that themes derived from students' interests and concerns can be powerful objects of study, but do not believe this should rule out teacher selection altogether. Taking Sasha's suggestion in future classes would mean ignoring the positive feedback of students who enjoyed studying anorexia, a topic most knew previously little or nothing about, such as Ana's, Maria's ("I preferred the topics about Dibs and Anorexia Nervosa because there were topics that are happening in today society"), and Carlos' ("An activity that I liked the most was studying in groups about the psychology course and learning about anorexia. It really was a interesting topic"). Attending to Sasha's suggestion would also deny an opportunity to balance the masculinist orientation of the psychology class.

My goal of introducing gender balance into the psychology class curriculum raises the issue of the role of the EAP teacher in curriculum development. The traditional EAP position perpetuates the lowly status of ESL teachers, mainly women, in higher education. If EAP teachers followed Horowitz's recommendation of only assigning topics and genres from the content course, their own intellectual contribution to the curriculum would be excluded. Fashioning EAP syllabi whose sole purpose is to support content courses goals, inevitably positions the EAP teacher in an anti-intellectual and subservient role, what Raimes (1991b) calls the "butler's stance" (p. 243).

Critical EAP, instead, positions EAP teachers as active intellectuals whose curricular goals extend beyond merely propping up content courses. Freire's (1998b) influence posits a strong role for teachers in constructing curricula to connect theory and practice. Critical teachers "cannot be effective when they remain in the thrall of an exploitative school system that robs them of their own voice," according to Aronowitz (1998, p. 13). In the EAP/psychology linked courses, I viewed myself as an equal partner, not a subordinate member of the team. Nor did the psychology professors position me in a subaltern role. Instead, they told me they hoped I would connect the material they taught to students' lives, by drawing on examples from their experience, and use the psychology topics as material for writing. I determined that if the women in my classes were to connect psychology to their lives, they would need at least one alternative to the masculinist psychology curriculum. Basing my decision on institutional and departmental goals and my own feminist and critical interests, I chose anorexia. My engagement with that topic sustained me throughout the 3 weeks of study, as the class developed their responses and projects. Yet, the traditional EAP literature overlooks the intellectual life of EAP teachers, assuming their job is to support the goals of the content course, even if those goals reduce academic life to listening, taking notes, memorizing definitions, and taking tests. I have not come across recommendations in the literature that EAP teachers find one area of study that interests them and promote that topic as an object of inquiry even though their intellectual engagement could be a great stimulus for students.

Although I seem to be expressing a preference for teacher selection in this final section of the chapter, revisiting anorexia has led me to conclude that critical EAP classes should offer flexibility about topic selection, leaving room for a variety of possibilities: teacher choice, student choice, and whole-class choice, in different combinations. There should be chances for the curriculum to emerge from students' questions about content classes and from their prior interests. There should also be collaborative decision making about what to study, to develop a greater sense of community and mutual responsibility.

I also hope that critical EAP teachers allow themselves to choose what they determine to be areas of inquiry, perhaps prompting rich dialogue, especially areas usually neglected by academic disciplines. Their choices do not have to please everyone. In fact, dissent about the teacher-selected topic could be an object of study in itself: Why do you oppose this topic? How is it different from the other subjects we studied? What would be a better choice? Why? Questions of this nature get at the social construction of curricula, why some topics are deemed more acceptable than others, and how those decisions are made. Yet, I would not want the opposition of a few students, such as George and Sasha, to dominate the discourse. After all, critical EAP teachers have institutional, social, and pedagogical perspectives, allowing them to make considered curricular judgements beyond the confines of a pragmatic approach to needs analysis. They are members of the academic community whose intellectual interests can help balance the curriculum.

Chapter 6

Building Community With Diversity: A Linked EAP/Anthropology Course

Distinguishing immigrant and international students as separate populations is a way to highlight differences between permanent residents who study in their adopted countries and temporary residents who earn degrees and return to their home countries. Awareness of possible disparities in the goals and backgrounds of the two populations has led to an increase in research on immigrant students who receive less attention than international students (Bosher & Rowenkamp, 1998; Harklau, Losey, & Siegal, 1999). However, the research reveals the difficulty of this type of sorting. One obstacle is that the multiple identities of students in both groups defy neat categorization. For example, Harklau, Losey, and Siegal (1999) find that immigrant students in the United States begin their schooling at different levels—elementary, junior high, or high school. Some may be highly educated on arrival; others have experienced interrupted schooling in their native countries. Their families come from various class backgrounds. Some have strong literacy skills in L1 and others do not. Their literacy skills in English also vary.

Nor are international students a uniform group. As Leki (1992) points out, some plan to get degrees and return home, while others seek permission to get an education abroad as a way to emigrate. Another distinction is that those from privileged backgrounds may be seeking an interesting adventure by studying abroad, yet those from more disadvantaged backgrounds may be pursuing economic opportunities not available at home.

Despite these findings, pointing to the complicated and overlapping identities of all non-native speaking students, resident status continues to be used as a means of classification in many U.S. colleges. An unanticipated effect of this sorting is that it has bolstered efforts to segregate immigrant and international students and offer different types of language instruction to members of those groups in some colleges. Segregationist policies apply the label "remedial students" to non-native permanent residents who are unable to demonstrate proficiency in L2 reading and writing. The assumption is that because they attended secondary school in the adopted country, these students should therefore be proficient in English before entering college. If they do not demonstrate proficiency by passing reading and writing tests, they may be deemed underprepared and channeled into precollege courses and institutes rather than academic ESL programs. International students, on the other hand, may be viewed a priori as better-prepared and therefore deserving of contextualized instruction in an academic ESL program. Their failing scores on language proficiency tests are viewed as indicators of a need for college-level ESL, not remediation or exclusion from academic programs.

The setting for this chapter is an anthropology course linked to an EAP writing course the students of which happened to be an almost-even number of immigrant and international students, an unusual occurrence in the City University of New York (CUNY) whose ESL population is predominantly permanent residents. This unexpected enrollment pattern forced me to test my own assumptions, throughout the semester, about the impact of resident status on academic performance. It also allowed me to explore Oakes' (1985) finding that heterogeneous grouping is beneficial for all students, an assumption at odds with the changing political climate at CUNY away from open admissions toward greater sorting and tracking, explained in the next section.

The course was an opportunity to challenge the categories of immigrant (remedial) and international (ESL) by encouraging students with varying experiences and strengths to collaborate on anthropology assignments and on improving conditions in that class. That is, the guiding principle was cooperation between students toward shaping and meeting the demands of the content course, not competition. It enacted Diamond and Quinby's (1988) proposal for "cooperation, community, and communion" (p. 204), a feminist response to individual competition and autonomy, by carrying out an experiment in community-building across class, ethnic, racial, and gender lines. This is not to say that those subject positions were disregarded but, rather, that the focus was on facing limit-situations collectively rather than privately. This notion of community is elaborated later in the chapter.

BACKGROUND: WHAT IS AN ESL STUDENT?

During the 1993–1994 academic year, the City University of New York set up a task force whose charge was to "make recommendations to the University for developing policy and funding programs for ESL students" (CUNY ESL Task Force Report, 1994, p. 2). One goal was to collect data about the university's ESL programs to "provide information on student success, progress, and instructional approaches" (p. 2). As task force members began to compile various data, they were faced with the question of how to define ESL students. Three criteria had been used previously by the university to identify these students: reporting less comfort using English than another language; birth in a country other than the United States; and reporting a language other than English as the native language. Finding these indicators misleading because they include students from other anglophone countries as well as bilingual students, the task force decided to define ESL students simply as those enrolled in ESL courses. This solution avoided offering a bureaucratic designation that would mask complicated identity and linguistic issues.

The question of how to identify ESL students arose again in 1998 when the university's board of trustees were formulating a plan to end remediation in the senior colleges, part of the changing political climate toward greater stratification, in the name of improving standards. Unsatisfied with the task force's definition of an ESL student as one who is enrolled in an ESL class, they came up with a different criterion. Those who had spent any part of their secondary education in a school outside the United States and did not pass CUNY's reading and/or writing placement tests would be considered ESL; those who had spent their entire secondary education in a United States high school and did not pass the tests would be considered remedial. Remedial students would have to enroll in a 2-year college, an associate's (2-year) degree program at a senior college offering that degree, or a precollege language immersion institute. ESL instruction in bachelor's degree programs at senior colleges would be reserved for the first group. The implications of this type of sorting are discussed next.

RESEARCH ON TRACKING

In *Keeping Track: How Schools Structure Inequality,* Oakes (1985) reports on the impact of tracking on 13,719 students in 297 classes in 25 junior and senior high schools across the United States. Oakes defines tracking as "the process whereby students are divided into categories so that they can be assigned in groups to various kinds of classes" (p. 3). Tracking, according to Oakes, is based not on empirical evidence but, rather, on four unexamined assumptions:

1. students do best when grouped with those who are believed to be similar to them academically;
2. so-called *slower* students develop more positive attitudes about themselves when not grouped with so-called *brighter* students;
3. there are valid placement measures that can sort students fairly into groups reflecting differences in proficiency and ability; and
4. tracking makes teaching more effective and classrooms more manageable.

Oakes' (1985) findings, based both on her reading of 60 years' of research on tracking and on her own study, challenge each of these assumptions. She found, for example, that "no group of students has been found to benefit consistently from being in a homogeneous group" (p. 7) and that lower-track students are more adversely affected due, in part, to the dumbed-down curriculum they are subject to: "high-track students got Shakespeare; low-track students got reading kits" (p. 192). Reviewing the second assumption, that slower students do better when protected from those who are academically stronger, she finds, instead, that tracking depresses the aspirations and damages the self-images of students placed in lower tracks. Responding to the third assumption related to placement measures, Oakes finds that although it is easy to develop tests that will sort students according to certain differences, it is not clear whether the particular differences being tested are predictive of future success nor whether they reflect the curriculum students will eventually face. She wonders, then, whether these instruments that measure relatively small differences between students are "appropriate criteria for separating students for instruction" (p. 11). Finally, in response to the fourth assumption that it is easier to teach students of similar educational backgrounds and achievements, Oakes finds this to be a self-fulfilling prophecy based on the ways schools are currently structured. Pointing out that the brightest students do well "regardless of the configuration of the groups they learn with" (p. 194) and that the slower students are harmed by the stigma and dumbed-down curricula of placement in low tracks, Oakes calls for heterogeneous classes in which all types of students interact in an intellectually challenging environment.

The linked course, discussed in this chapter, presented an opportunity to create such an environment. Before exploring that course, however, I define what I mean by community and community-building as used in the chapter's title and introduction, and relate these concepts to the benefits of heterogeneous grouping claimed by Oakes.

COMMUNITY AND A PEDAGOGY OF DIFFERENCE

The term *community* as used here requires further elaboration due to its evocation in a variety of settings, including frequent references in the EAP literature to discourse communities. My use of community is distinguished from EAP's traditional definition in important ways. In the EAP literature, academic discourse communities are assumed to have a hierarchical structure based on a distinction between novices and experts. Outsiders are expected to be socialized by insiders in order for membership to be achieved. In EAP, that means that professors are considered experts whose discourse practices are to be adopted by students in order for them to be initiated into the community. Membership is contingent on students surrendering their discourse to that of the experts. Aside from these membership requirements, discourse communities are also assumed to be formed around a "broadly agreed set of common public goals" (Swales, 1990, p. 24).

The sense in which I am using community, to the contrary, is not based on a notion of hierachy or induction of novices by experts. Instead, it is founded on a postmodern recognition of difference (Weiler, 1994), of multiple and overlapping identities and goals. Yet, the recognition of difference does not rule out the possibility of shared needs and rights among people who find themselves together temporarily, like students in a class. In the case of the linked courses described in this book, students are placed in them because of failing scores on proficiency tests. That is, they do not voluntarily join a discourse community into which they would like to be socialized, as graduate students might do. Rather, they enroll in courses whose purposes include preparing to pass the proficiency tests, improving in reading and writing, and understanding content-course material.

Although students in these courses do not share a common identity and purpose in these courses, they face limit-situations in the courses that impede them to varying degrees. For example, passing proficiency tests and fulfilling the requirements of the content course are limit-situations, creating a temporary common purpose among students whose future academic goals may differ considerably. In a critical EAP classroom, those shared limit-situations can become the grounds for cooperation and community building, moving from private fulfillment of assignments to collective work for the benefit of all students, including possibly challenging unreasonable requirements. The linked course format offers many opportunities to cultivate community due to the amount of time students spend together in the two classes.

Beyond the local issue of community in the specific linked EAP writing/anthropology course discussed here, a larger political question about community and diversity is faced by critical teachers trying both to promote equity and to honor the complexity of multiple identities. It is about "identify[ing] and struggl[ing] to achieve collective goals and moral imperatives across boundaries of social identity" (Morgan, 1998, p. 18). The twin aims of "coalition building" and "recognition and validation of difference" (Weiler, 1994, p. 35) preoccupy critical teachers who refuse to abandon the hope of greater social equality although they gladly shed the modernist assumption of universal emancipation. McLaren (1994), citing JanMohamed (1993) describes this relationship as "disidentification" to distance oneself from overdetermined and fixed identities and "reidentification" (p. 206) to form new affiliations in the interest of greater social equity. So, for example, in this chapter, I discuss one student, Francesca, who was accustomed to assuming a good-student position, someone who knew how to query her teachers about assignments to get what she needed for herself, to fulfill assignments. Yet, when challenged by fellow EAP students about why she worked exclusively on her own behalf, she began to reconsider her position as an autonomous player and to cooperate with others on assignments. This and other examples of community-building are discussed next.

SETTING: A LINKED EAP WRITING/ANTHROPOLOGY COURSE

The EAP course was linked to an introduction to anthropology course. About half the students enrolled in anthropology were also taking my EAP writing class; the others were not enrolled in any linked class. Cultural anthropology was the focus of three quarters of the anthropology course and human evolution was the topic of the final weeks. Professor Gold, the anthropology teacher and I met two times before the semester began to develop a syllabus. The main textbook she proposed, Robbins (1997) *Cultural Anthropology: A Problem-Oriented Approach,* offered interesting exercises designed for students to interrogate their thinking about family, traditions, beliefs, identity, gender, and so on. As a supplemental text, I proposed *Anthropology 97/98* from the Annual Editions series (Angeloni, 1997), a collection of articles from magazines and newspapers on topics in cultural anthropology. These two texts formed the basis of instruction in both the anthropology and EAP classes, along with Tattersal's (1995), *The Fossil Trail,* Gold's choice for the human evolution text.

Professor Gold had great respect and high expectations for the students. Understanding the importance of writing as a way of learning, due in part to her participation in the English department's Developmental Education Study Group (see chap. 8), she included three major writing assignments on the original syllabus, as well as several short writing exercises. She also wanted students to participate in class discussions with questions and examples connecting the abstract concepts of anthropology to their own experience. However, several factors, discussed next, prevented that type of dialogue, causing frustration for students and teachers. The EAP class was an arena for dealing with these limit-situations and developing ways to achieve greater dialogue. Community formation became an important tool in trying to bring about a more satisfying experience in anthropology, one that invited participation rather than alienation and exclusion. It was a place for students to organize themselves to create a more conducive environment for engaged learning.

The EAP Writing Class

The 18 students in the EAP writing class were from a wide range of national backgrounds: two Albanians; one Belizean; one Brazilian; one Dominican; one Filipino; one Greek; two Haitians; one Honduran; one Italian; one Jamaican; one Malagasy; three Nigerians; one Pakistani; and one Sri Lankan. Four of these students could have been transferred to a class for native speakers of English, yet chose to remain in ESL to avoid disrupting their schedules or because they were more comfortable studying with non-natives. For example, although Ann had emigrated from Jamaica 11 years before, she had not questioned her ESL placement during registration because she believed the linked course would help her pass the writing assessment test she had previously failed several times at a CUNY community college. Fidelia, from Nigeria, reported English as her first language but she had been in the United States only 1 month when she enrolled at the college, so she preferred to be in a class with other non-natives. Edward, a fluent English speaker, had emigrated to the United States from Belize 20 years before but was in his mid-30s and had been out of school for many years while raising a family. Although he was ambivalent about being in ESL, the linked courses fit his schedule and so he remained. Jusuf was born in the United States to Albanian parents, and was misplaced in ESL, but he decided to stay rather than reorganize his schedule to accommodate a class for natives. His enthusiastic participation in the classes was a great benefit.

Seven students had earned diplomas from high schools outside the United States: Elena, from Greece who had been in the United States only 1 month; Magdalena, from Brazil, who had also recently arrived; Francesca, whose family had emigrated from Italy 2 years before; Sabri, from Albania, another recent arrival; Alain, whose family had come from Madagascar via France 2 years before, and two brothers from Nigeria, Olu and Ade, whose parents shuttled between businesses in England, Nigeria, and the United States while their sons studied.

The other eight students reported a first language other than English, yet all of them had United States high school diplomas, two having started school in the United States in elementary school, one in junior high, and the other in high school. Looking at the various placement criteria, length of time in the United States, high school diploma, first language, and so on, it is understandable why the CUNY ESL Task Force opted to define ESL students as those enrolled in ESL classes. This criterion acknowledges the complexity of the question and the difficulty of sorting students into native and non-native categories. It also allows for a certain amount of self-selection by students who prefer to be placed with non-natives even if, like Jusuf, they were born in the U.S. but spoke a language other than English at home.

The heterogeneity of the EAP class allowed for community-building in ways that might not have been possible if ESL were defined as the exclusive domain of students who had attended secondary schools outside the United States. In particular, exchanges between students of varying class backgrounds would not have taken place because, generally speaking, students residing temporarily in the United States for study purposes are wealthier than those who emigrate. Also lost would have been exchanges between recent arrivals and long-term residents whose varied experiences were a strength of this particular class.

COMMUNITY FORMATION IN THE EAP CLASS

Feminist proposals for "cooperation, community, and communion" (Diamond & Quinby, 1988, p. 204) offer an alternative to autonomous notions of empowerment that sometimes appear in the critical pedagogy literature. Yet without descriptions of how community formation comes about, including lapses and missed opportunities, proposals for cooperation remain abstract ideals. Moving from abstract notions of community to the concrete daily operations of a classroom striving for cooperation, this chapter offers a description of ways EAP students worked together to understand, question, and shape the material and assignments of the anthropology class.

One of the challenges of encouraging community in the EAP class was to problematize my preconceptions about preparation for college work. I had to interrogate my own tendency to assume that international students, graduates of non-U.S. high schools, would be better prepared than permanent residents, and I then had to question the meaning of preparation. CUNY's placement exams in reading and writing construct preparation as testable skills (Benesch, 1991). Students are deemed proficient by virtue of having passed the tests and assumed to be ready for college-level courses. The assessment is based on what Johns (1997) calls a "naive" theory positing literacy as a "unitary macroskill" (p. 73). Although the tests are relied on to make judgements about who may be mainstreamed and who may not, they do not reflect the type of work asked of students in the content courses I have observed, including listening to lectures, taking notes, reading a professor's notes on the chalkboard, reading text books, and studying for exams. Also, the courses themselves vary considerably, due to the idiosyncracies of the teachers, an observation made by Prior (1995), Leki (1995), and Spack (1997) in their ethnographic studies of college courses. So, what does it mean for a non-native speaking student to be prepared for academic course work in a U.S. college? If literacy is not simply a unitary macroskill, achieved once and for all, and if each target situation presents unique challenges, what does it mean to be prepared for those situations? If preparation is not a foundational set of skills allowing students to perform well in all academic settings, what is it?

Rather than basing instruction on the notion that some students (those educated outside the United States) would more easily meet the challenges than others (those educated in New York City public schools), I began to ask what type of preparation was required for *anyone,* myself included, to be a student of introductory anthropology with this particular teacher. Then, shifting the focus from subgroups or categories of students (immigrant vs. international) to the class as a whole, I wondered how as a group they could equip themselves together to deal with the requirements of this specific content class. I turned my attention away from the advantages a particular kind of secondary education might have created for some, realizing that focusing on that variable might interfere with my ability to address the particular limit-situations this linked course presented. Instead, I concentrated on how strengths shown by individual students in each of the classes could be called on to benefit the entire EAP class. That is, while I continued to see the students as individuals, I began to consider their personal and academic attributes as potential contributions to the group, not as private credentials.

Clearly, some of the students were better readers than others. They kept up with the textbook reading and were able to make connections between the reading and lectures. Others gave up more quickly when encountering unfamiliar terms in the text or losing track of the meaning during one of the anthropology lectures. So, the EAP class devoted the bulk of its time to making sense of the reading and lectures and the connections between them by reviewing students' notes and discussing content.

As important as these pragmatic activities were, there was also the need to cultivate a sense of membership so that all students felt that they belonged in the institution and the classes as subjects of learning, not objects of teaching. Two students, Elena and Francesca, graduates of Greek and Italian high schools, respectively, had that sense of belonging with no intervention on my part. They participated comfortably in anthropology class discussions from the beginning, exhibiting no fear of speaking in front of the other students or of appearing foolish if they asked clarifying questions. For example, during the second anthropology class meeting, after Professor Gold asked a question about the reading they had done at home, Elena said, unapologetically, "I don't understand the question." Her desire to understand overrode any possible concern she might have had about offending the teacher, a feature of her composure I wanted other students to acquire. That is, the sense of entitlement allowing Elena and Francesca to participate openly in the anthropology class was something I hoped to engender in the others. They emerged as class leaders who could inspire others to claim membership.

A discussion during the third week of the semester about how to increase verbal participation in the anthropology class revealed that students had various reasons for keeping quiet. Prompted by Gold's remark to me that she would like more verbal contributions from students during her classes, to create a more interactive climate, I asked the EAP students why only a few of them joined in the classroom conversation. One student explained, "It's dangerous. If we ask a question she might go off for a half-hour." Another added, "She'll get lost." It seemed that Gold's informal lecturing style made some of them nervous and they therefore tried not to contribute to a lack of continuity by asking questions, even when they lost track of points being made. This observation led to a discussion about the relationship between the lectures and students' notes. I suggested that if their notes kept up with the progress of the lecture, students could consult them to remind themselves and, if necessary, the teacher where she had left off before going on a tangent. Note-taking in this context was seen not only as a private record of lecture material but also as a collective effort to get the lecture on track, a possible benefit for others.

With reading and lecture notes considered community property, students were encouraged to improve their note-taking so that they could take responsibility for the lectures' smoother progress and each others' comprehension. What emerged during discussions of note-taking was that most students did not know what to write when listening to a lecture; they could not always pick out the main points. They therefore asked for advice about what to write down and shared notes to compare various ways of doing it. Developing solutions to these problems was a communal undertaking. No one's prior experience in secondary school had prepared them for Gold's lecturing style with its unpredictable twists and turns. For the most part, they enjoyed the material and wanted to understand it more completely but were often stymied by an absence of verbal signals that could have underscored the significance of certain points and their relationship to previous material, or highlighted the introduction of new material. Without those signals, students often stopped listening and started whispering to each other. To promote greater attention in the anthropology class, I asked students to work with each other in the EAP class on reconstructing the previous lecture and to make connections with the related reading. One result of the more attentive note-taking was that after Professor Gold had finished answering questions during a lecture, EAP students were able to reorient themselves, and sometimes Gold herself, to the main topic.

A contrast to ways the EAP students were organizing themselves to improve conditions in the anthropology class was the way a group of four native English-speaking students enrolled in the course, but not in a linked class, reacted to the lectures. These four young men frequently carried on audible conversations with each other while Gold was lecturing. Although Gold did not seem concerned about the ongoing student chat during lectures, I was both distracted by their talking and curious about why it was happening. Therefore, one day after the anthropology class, I approached the four young men and asked them why they spoke to each other during class. After some hesitation, during which they stared shyly at their shoes, one said, "We're bored." Another said, "I've never taken anthropology before. I don't know what she's talking about." I asked them if there might be an alternative to talking to each other when they did not understand the lecture. One offered that it might be more useful to ask questions, perhaps because they had noticed EAP students' questions. In fact, two of the four young men began to ask questions from time to time, but the chatting continued, offering an interesting contrast to EAP students' interventions with questions and references to their notes. This is not to say that the EAP students were fully engaged at all moments. However, their membership in a community seemed to have offered a more positive way to respond to the challenging conditions of the anthropology class than by chatting, the principle mode of resistance of the four young men in the face of incomprehension and alienation.

Lectures were not the only challenge for students. In addition, they had to navigate assignment guidelines, including changing due dates. In the following section, I explore how the EAP class functioned as a community to help each other with the guidelines.

Making Sense of Assignments Together

Prior (1995), Leki (1995), and Spack (1997) demonstrate that assignments are not simply a set of teacher-made guidelines to be faithfully followed by students. Instead, their research shows how students negotiate various aspects of assignments both before beginning them and as they carry them out. As far as understanding the tasks themselves, Prior (1995) found that this was a difficult undertaking "as the professor frequently restated or alluded to them in ways that suggest subtle and not-so-subtle differences and as students frequently initiated implicit and explicit negotiation over the tasks" (p. 53). Carrying out assignments was not, as he had expected it to be, just a matter of students "attempting to passively match the professor's expectations" (p. 53). Instead, task-setting, fulfillment, and evaluation were situated in the dynamics of particular classes and influenced by a complex set of social and intellectual variables. Like Prior's subjects, students in the EAP class involved themselves in a process of understanding and negotiating writing assignments. However, the focus of my teaching and research was not how individual students negotiated with Gold but how the class worked together to clarify and do assignments.

One challenge was that Gold periodically revised the syllabus, sometimes confusing students about when assignments were due. This issue arose during an EAP class meeting when Jusuf asked about the due date for one of the anthropology assignments. Francesca answered, "Oh, I asked her [Gold]. She said it's due on . . ." and she gave the date. In reference to Francesca's answer, Patrick, a Haitian student, said, "She went for herself. She should go for the whole class," perhaps acknowledging that the class was a community and that the ethos was to help each other rather than only oneself.[8] Everyone could have benefitted from the information Francesca

---

[8]The issue of individualism vs. collectivism was not one we had explicitly discussed in the EAP class. In future linked courses I might initate discussion of the differences between working for oneself and working for the group, especially to discover students' varying reactions to community-building.

had acquired, Patrick seemed to be saying. Then Edward, the student from Belize, asked Francesca, "Why don't you ask her at the beginning of class instead of at the end?" His question suggested that if Francesca or another student queried Gold before the lecture began rather than after the class was over, the information would be available to all the students.

This exchange about due dates led to a larger discussion about how the students might help each other not only reconstruct lectures, as they were used to doing, but also deconstruct and carry out assignments. One solution proposed by Edward and accepted by the others was that those who felt most comfortable asking about assignments in class would do so and that those who felt more comfortable asking privately would share the information with the other students as soon as possible. Not only did this discussion solidify the burgeoning sense of community, it also encouraged more students to ask Gold for clarification of assignment guidelines during her class. Here is an example of students trying to make sense of the human evolution assignment during the eighth week of anthropology:

(On the board, Gold writes a list of journals and a sample citation of an article from one of the journals. She explains that students are to find three articles in three different anthropology or science journals about human evolution and write a five-page review).

Edward: Can you give us a list of topics?

Gold: No, you get to choose your own topic.

Edward: OK. But once we do that, can you give us the structure of how we present the articles?

Gold: Summarize the main argument of each article. (On the board, she writes the following guidelines:

  I. What is the topic?
  II. What seem to be the main differences of opinion about the topic?
  III. For each article: a. Summarize the main position of the authors.
     b. What evidence do they use to support their position?
     c. How convincing is it? Do you see any problems with their position?)

Edward: Based on our own opinion?

Shazhad: Do we do it together on the page? We don't have to do it on three sheets?

Gold: No, it's a paper. You write it in paragraphs. The articles will point out problems with the arguments. You don't really have to rely on your own judgment. (She continues to write on the board:

IV. Pick the position that seems most likely (or congenial or best-argued) that you like the best and tell me why).

Francesca: You want it about human evolution, but do you want it a specific age? There is stuff from 100 years ago.

Gold: That's a good question. I want it from the earliest evidence of modern humans, from the earliest evidence of Australopithecines.

Georges: Can you choose articles from different journals?

Gold: That's what library research is. Going through the literature to find articles on the same topic. When you do research you want to find out what others have done so you don't re-invent the wheel. You want to know what's been done.

Student from unlinked section: So we're just getting three articles and comparing them?

Gold: You can probably do it in five concise pages. Make an outline using this as a framework. Put key words in the outline that organize your thoughts.

Jorge: When is this due?

Gold: During exam week. You have a lot of time. Of course we haven't gone over this material in class. . . . Are there any questions on patterns of family relationships?

This excerpt reveals three types of questions about assignments: process, structure, and content. Edward's questions are of the first type: He asks for guidance on how to carry out the research and writing. He wants advice about each stage of the process from topic selection to presenting the data, including how, as a student, he should relate to the writing of professional anthropologists ("Based on our own opinion?"). Shahzad's question about whether to separate the information on the three articles or keep it together on one page is about structure. Francesca is concerned mainly with content, wondering what period of prehistory the assignment aimed to capture. More difficult to interpret is George's question about choosing articles from different journals because that requirement is specifically stated in the guidelines. I believe his query was an attempt to integrate all the instructions as he faced a task he had never carried out before. Indeed, Gold's response very helpfully put the assignment in the context of doing research. Rather than dismissing his question as one that was answered in the guidelines, she explained the purpose of reading articles on the same topic: "to find out what others have done." Jorge's question about the due date may have been a reflection of the frequent revisions of the syllabus, mentioned earlier. Perhaps by asking her to say the date out loud, he was trying to exact a commitment from her.

However, due dates were not the only ambiguous aspect of assignments. At times, students were not clear about whether papers would be collected at all, especially when due dates had passed and Gold had not asked for them. The issue of collecting assignments whose due dates had passed arose when, unexpectedly, Gold announced a new assignment not listed in the syllabus: a required visit to the American Museum of Natural History's human evolution exhibit. The announcement and students' reactions to it are discussed in the next section.

THE DELEGATION

Three weeks after making the research assignment and 3 weeks before the end of the semester, Gold told the students they were required to go the human evolution exhibit at the American Museum of Natural History in Manhattan and write one or two pages on their impression of one of the displays. She then wrote directions for travel by public transportation from the college to the museum. Students asked several questions about the relationship between this new assignment, the previous one, and the reading that had been assigned on human evolution. For example, Francesca asked, "Our museum paper—we have to talk about what we see and we have to talk about the relationship to the book?" Gold then explained the museum assignment in more detail: "Just write a response to the exhibit, free writing. Stop at the case and ask 'What have I learned that I didn't know before?' There's lots of stuff. Origins of cave art . . ." She then suggested possible displays on which they might concentrate.

When students arrived in the EAP class during the following period, they were talking about the museum visit. Elena expressed her indignation: "We have 20 days left to do all this work. Why didn't she make the museum assignment when we had 10 days off for spring break? So far only two assignments have been due. Two assignments in 3 months. Now in the last month of class she gives us these new assignments not on the syllabus." Not wanting to take a position and wanting to see how students would frame the problem Elena had articulated, I asked them to detail the list of assignments due between then and the end of the semester. As they called out the assignments, I wrote them on the board. They were: folk tale paper, soap opera paper, museum visit, museum paper, final research paper on three articles, read four chapters of Tattersal, and take-home quiz on Tattersal. After the list was on the board, I asked how the class wanted to deal with it. Elena suggested they ask Gold to cancel the museum visit saying, "We have no time; we're in class everyday." She also said that she had wanted to suggest eliminating the museum visit during the anthropology class but had decided that it was not effective for one person to speak up.

Based on Elena's observation that one person protesting was less effective than a group and on a sense that the number of assignments due was presenting an unreasonable demand on students' time and limited experience with anthropology, I suggested forming a delegation to work on a solution and present a proposal to Gold. Four students immediately volunteered: Elena, Francesca, Jusuf, and Jorge. I asked Georges to join them, knowing that he had cultivated a relationship with Gold by asking her for help outside of class with his papers, indicating that he was less confident in the EAP class' collaborative style than other students. I then encouraged the delegation to work out how they would negotiate with Gold, in consultation with the other students, and what they would try to accomplish. Elena suggested that they ask her to drop the museum visit and paper. Georges, on the other hand, objected more to the soap opera paper: "I didn't think we had to do the soap opera paper because, according to the syllabus, it was due on March 23." (It was then late April). After further discussion with the class, the delegation met, formulated their proposal, and went to Gold's office to talk it over with her. They asked me to join them, but I encouraged them to meet with Gold on their own, believing that the experience would be more satisfying if they carried out their plan without me.

The result of the delegation's visit, announced by Gold at the beginning of the next anthropology class meeting, was that she would drop the soap opera assignment but keep the museum visit, explaining that it would help them understand the Tattersal (1995) book on human evolution. She also encouraged the students to choose together which part of the exhibit they would write about and then to do the writing collaboratively. That is, she not only offered a convincing rationale for the assignment but also diminished students' concerns about the extent of the work by making it more informal. The EAP students were pleased with what had been accomplished. The elimination of the soap opera paper freed them to concentrate more closely on the other assignments and the modification of the museum paper allowed them to work with each other, rather than in isolation. They were also gratified that they had been received so graciously by Gold, who listened carefully to their concerns and responded to them reasonably and fairly. They set aside their fears about traveling to the museum and having extra work. Gold later told me that she had been surprised but pleased by the delegation's arrival at her office and the care they had taken to negotiate a solution with her.

THE MUSEUM VISIT: MIRANDA'S QUESTIONS

Never having visited the human evolution exhibit myself and wanting to interact with the EAP students outside the campus setting, I decided to join them at the American Museum of Natural History on the day they planned to go together. They arrived in groups of three, four, and five, having taken a bus, a ferry, and a subway during a torrential rainstorm. They circulated among the displays, choosing one to focus on in pairs or small groups. I went from group to group, trying to answer questions, though my limited knowledge about evolution prevented me from offering much beyond what was described in the texts accompanying the exhibits. The restriction on the amount of help I could offer was driven home to me most clearly by two questions from Miranda, the Dominican student. She, Olu, and Ade arrived a little later than the others and were having trouble settling on a particular display to write about. I walked around with them from case to case suggesting different topics. As we stood in front of the "Humans are Primates" display, Miranda paused for a while to look at the large mural of primates in trees, climbing, playing, and eating, in a lush landscape with a river and mountains in the background. One of the panels she read included the following text:

> Together with the monkeys of the Old and New Worlds, and the lesser and great apes, humans are informally classified as "higher" primates. More technically, we all belong to a suborder of primates called Anthropoidea or Haplorhini.

A side panel, next to the mural included this sentence: "The details of our anatomical structure reveal our common heritage with the other members of the order Primates: the lemur, lorises, tarsiers, monkeys and apes." Under this text, was a graphic of a young woman surrounded by various primates.

After studying the display, Miranda asked me, "Do we really come from the apes? Does that mean an ape could become a human?" The fact that the human evolution exhibit provoked these questions, ones it was designed to answer, created an interesting challenge. Even if I had been able to provide learned responses to Miranda's questions, they seemed to be calling out for more than direct answers based on familiarity with the subject matter. The questions required exploring what might have led Miranda to ask them in the first place. Was she experiencing conflicts between what she saw in the display and what she had learned at home or elsewhere? What was her understanding of the relationship between humans and animals, and how did it relate to what she was looking at in the human evolution exhibit? With no experience handling this kind of question, and not being sure what kind they were, I wondered how to help her reconcile her previous knowledge with the findings presented in the exhibit. It was a moment that reminded me of the limitations of an EAP teacher faced with issues outside her area of expertise, one discussed by Spack (1988), in her article, "Initiating students into the academic discourse community: How far should we go?" In that article, (discussed in chap. 3), Spack raises concerns about English teachers' "lack of control over content" (p. 37) they find themselves in the position of having to explain. Not only will the teacher feel uncomfortable, she asserts, but they may be unable to "recognize when a student failed to demonstrate adequate knowledge of a discipline or showed a good grasp of new knowledge" (p. 37).

Yet, my problem with Miranda's questions were not only that I lacked control over the human evolution content but also that, not being an anthropology teacher, I had not anticipated Miranda's questions as ones that might be commonly asked by students who are new to anthropology. I was therefore unprepared to explore the questions' subtexts, the deeper issues embedded within them. Not knowing how to address the questions beyond a simple "yes" to the first and "no" to the second, I encouraged Miranda to ask Professor Gold to answer them more completely in class, hoping that her long experience with students' questions about evolution, including possible conflicts with creationism, would address Miranda's hidden concerns.

Gold's in-class answers to Miranda's questions were contained within a lecture on Darwin and challenges to his theory of evolution, reconstructed here from notes I took during the lecture:

> Darwin speculated that he could explain the appearance of animal bones in ancient deposits resembling modern species, but not the same. He sus-pected the fossil species were very old—Darwin said 100,000 to 1 million years. Christian theologians' manipulations of Biblical texts prior to the birth of Christ calculated 3,000 to 4,000 years. That's the number of gener-ations in the Bible. That didn't leave enough time, doesn't leave room for fossils—layers with no evidence of human occupation. Early fossil layers were during times when no humans existed—prehuman. The timetable of creation is problematic. There's a tradition in Biblical interpretation of us-ing the stories as symbolic texts. Taking powerful stories and the imagery adds depth to the meaning. There are multiple levels of meaning, the way you do in the folktales. The Bible is not about biology. It's about peoples' relationship to each other, metaphors of nature. There's a conflict between science and religion. The Bible isn't about evolution; it's about social rules.

> We share the same genes as every living thing—fruit flies, plants. 99.2% of chimp DNA is exactly the same as human. Both descended from a common ancestor 6 million years ago. The material is the same, arranged differ-ently. Genes don't control what you see. The genotype is the stable struc-ture, the underlying design instruction (If your parents are chimps, you'll be a chimp). The phenotype is what develops, variation and flexibility. There's potential for variation in the phenotype, especially behavior. The phenotype is a flexible rendering depending on the development of the genotype.

After making these statements, Gold summarized Darwin's theory of natural selection, including examples of the breeding habits of wolves and the evolution of long necks and legs in giraffes. This was followed by challenges to Darwin, particularly the lack of explanation of stability:

> The problem with Darwin's story is you had to account not just for mutability, gradual change. You also had to account for stability. Why aren't things chang-ing all the time? Why don't we have transitions from monkeys to humans? Why did the intermediaries die out? The Ape and Human are still living. Why did the intermediary forms die out?

In the final part of this lecture, Gold discussed Mendel and the neo-Darwinian synthesis, to answer the questions she had just raised about stability.

Given the amount of new and abstract material presented, this was a particularly challenging lecture. Students listened closely and took notes, yet I wondered if Miranda was making connections between her questions and the information being offered on Darwin, the Bible, DNA, genotypes, phenotype, and so on. Normally, the following EAP class would have been devoted to making these connections but, unfortunately, there was no chance because the students had to prepare for the upcoming retest of the writing proficiency exam they had to pass in order to continue on to freshman composition the following semester. The opportunity to raise Miranda's question with the other students and explore their subtexts was therefore lost. Also lost was the chance to process the notes and lecture and make apparent the ways Gold had answered the questions. On my own as EAP teacher, I was not equipped to show Miranda the connections between her questions and the lecture. The anthropology lecture, though intended, in part, to answer Miranda's questions did not explicitly draw the connection between them and the new material presented. To take Miranda into account would have required that the EAP class work together, focusing its attention on the specific concerns she had raised. Her membership in that community might have guided the activities, benefitting those who participated in clarifying their understanding of important and complicated questions.

ACCESS AND COMMUNITY

Miranda's questions point to the relationship between access and community in critical EAP. As a student who had emigrated to the United States from the Dominican Republic 10 years before enrolling in college and who had graduated from a New York City high school, Miranda would, under more restrictive segregationist policies, be considered a remedial student. That means she would not have access to credit-bearing content courses, like anthropology, where she would be offered challenging academic material on entry to college. Nor would she be in a heterogeneous class allowing her to observe the behavior of the strongest students and participate in conversations with a diverse group. Instead, she might instead be placed in precollege reading and writing courses, delaying her access to college and to academic content.

At the end of the semester, Miranda passed the writing assessment test required for entry to freshman composition and other credit-bearing courses. That is, she fulfilled a criterion for membership as a college student, but her college courses may not be prepared for her. She may find herself in lecture courses requiring memorization of material she does not fully understand. In that case, she might, like Leki's (1999) subject Jan, a permanent resident student enrolled at a public U.S. university, learn to cynically play the academic game of memorizing information without letting it touch or engage her. Without a community of peers to raise questions, promote greater dialogue, and voice their concerns about assignments, Miranda may find herself isolated and alienated. Or, she might organize with fellow students to form a study group, based on her experience in the linked course.

One carryover from the paired anthropology/EAP classes gives hope. Students in that community remained friends, signing up for the same courses in subsequent semesters, included one taught by Gold, staying in touch by phone, and meeting in the library to study together, a difficult achievement in a public college whose students commute and hold jobs. Their mutual support sustained them even in courses whose material they found abstract and inaccessible. It seems then, that enduring relationships can be part of community formation. Their role in retaining students is another area requiring further research.

SUMMARY

According to Otheguy (1999), testing and tracking policies formulated by the CUNY Board of Trustees in 1998 are part of a broader political agenda to keep immigrants in low-skill, low-pay jobs. In his view, excluding non-native speaking permanent residents from senior colleges because of failing scores on proficiency tests is an effort to depress the aspirations of new immigrants. "The intention of this policy is for the immigrant to go through one generation of taxi driving" (Otheguy, 1999).

Otheguy (1999) recommends reversing the usual construction of failure as a shortcoming of students to that of institutional inadequacy: "The problem is not a lack of success of ESL students; it's a lack of success of the university" in teaching these students. He also believes that linked courses are a way to preserve open admissions by mainstreaming students while offering language and content instruction concurrently.

The linked course described in this chapter was an experiment in community-building with students of diverse class, educational, and language backgrounds. As the community developed, students worked together to make sense of new material, keep the lectures on track, and clarify assignment guidelines. Deep and lasting friendships were formed that endured beyond the end of the semester, as students sought membership for themselves in the college. They needed each other's varying strengths to face the difficulties of academic study, especially in a climate of exclusion.

Although other institutions may not operate in the same political landscape as the one described here, sorting and tracking of non-native students is prevalent throughout the United States and other countries. Yet, EAP has not problematized tracking, perhaps having accepted the four assumptions outlined by Oakes (1985) in her critique of segregating students of varying educational backgrounds from each other. Two areas of research are suggested by questions raised about tracking in this chapter: The political processes by which students are placed into different tracks and offered different types of instruction, and the dynamics of heterogeneous classes in which students of differing strengths collaborate, the focus of this chapter.

Recognizing that tracking is a political process may also lead to greater attention in EAP to learners' social and economic needs as well as to their linguistic and cognitive ones. To facilitate this recognition, a nuanced approach to needs analysis in EAP, one balanced with rights analysis, must be considered. This the topic of the next chapter.

Chapter 7

Rights Analysis in a Paired
EAP/Psychology Lecture Class[9]

The previous chapter offere d an example of a paired EAP writing/anthropology course in which students worked collectively to meet the limit-situations presented by abstract material and ambiguous assignment guidelines. Implied in that example was needs analysis, that is, discovering target demands. Also implied was rights analysis, keeping open the possibility of challenging unreasónable requirements and conditions (Benesch, 1999a). However, the focus here is more directly on the relationship between needs and rights analysis, to explore critical EAP's role in balancing target requirements and student dissent.

To frame this discussion, I briefly review changes in the EAP literature regarding needs analysis and then compare and problematize needs and rights analysis.

NEEDS ANALYSIS

Needs analysis in EAP consists of gathering data about the target situation as the basis for designing EAP courses and materials. Whereas the definition of needs in the early years of ESP was limited to discrete linguistics items required by the target situation, affective and cognitive factors are now sometimes taken into account as well (Dudley-Evans & St. John, 1998; Hutchinson & Waters, 1987). Comprehensive needs analyses may therefore include not only target situation analysis but also learning-situation analysis and present-situation analysis—that is, what students know and do not know about the target subject (Dudley-Evans & St. John, 1998).

Building learning processes and students' prior knowledge into needs analysis is a welcome development. However, sociopolitical factors, such as

---

[9]An earlier version of this chapter appeared as an article in *English for Specific Purposes* (Benesch, 1999b).

gender, class, race, and power relations have yet to be taken into account when developing ESP/EAP curricula. This limitation was noted by Swales (1994) in his foreword to the final issue of *English for Specific Purposes*. According to Swales, the omission is due to ESP's "pragmatic tradition . . . trying to deliver maximum assistance in minimum time" (p. 201). Dudley-Evans and St. John (1998) attribute the lack of attention to social issues in needs analysis to the analyst's subjectivity. Identification and analysis of needs "depend on who asks what questions and how the responses are interpreted. What we ask and how we interpret are dependent on a particular view of the world, on attitudes and values" (p. 126). The dominant worldview, or ideology, of needs analysis in EAP has been to assume that target requirements are the goal, setting the purpose of instruction. This pragmatic tradition has excluded questioning requirements or engaging students in their reformulation (Benesch, 1993).

However, as the notion of context has expanded in EAP beyond cognitive and linguistic demands to include social issues and identities, the literature has begun to acknowledge this broader perspective (Dudley-Evans & St. John, 1998; Master, 1998; Swales, 1994). This chapter explores the relationship between needs analysis, pragmatic responses to target demands, and rights analysis. It is a study of power relations to discover alternatives to strict pragmatism and obedience to requirements.

PROBLEMATIZING NEEDS

The use of *needs analysis* to describe a tool for gathering data about institutional expectations is problematic for several reasons, some of which have been mentioned in previous chapters. First, it conflates external requirements and students' desires as if they were congruent, not a possible area of struggle. Second, it hides the ideological battles that go on in academic life around curricular decision-making by highlighting only the final outcomes of those charged decisions. When only the end results are taken into account, as they are in needs analysis, students receive an adulterated and simplified version of academic life, a point made Mahala (1991)[10] in his critique of the conservative tendencies of writing-across-the-curriculum (WAC) programs in U.S. universities. Third, it supports a notion of education as need fulfillment, based on a

---

[10]Mahala (1991) raises concerns about the "formalist school" of U.S. WAC programs that, he claims, stress "normative ways of arguing and gathering evidence in the disciplines" rather than "foregrounding tensions between competing, often mutually exclusive, strategies of knowledge-making" (p. 779). In response to Mahala's and others' disappointment with WAC's timidity in questioning business as usual, McLeod and Maimon (2000) claim that the movement has been "profoundly transformative" and that the changes have been "from the grassroots rather than by storming the barricades" (p. 578), although Mahala's critique of WAC does not include suggestions for fomenting campus revolution.

theory of cultural deprivation (Giroux, 1997). Students, according to this theory, are deprived and therefore require enrichment to achieve a better life. They are empty vaults into which knowledge must be deposited, Freire's (1970) famous metaphor of traditional education as banking. In the banking model, students are expected to "adapt to the world as it is and to the fragmented view of reality deposited in them" (p. 54). Missing from the cultural deficit theory and banking model is the recognition that the needs legitimated in schools "often represent the endorsement of a particular way of life" (Giroux, 1997, p. 127) not a neutral set of skills. By not acknowledging that the choice of what to teach is political, the needs-fulfillment model excludes students from participating in curriculum construction and reform.)

It could be argued that EAP specialists, due to their contact with non-native speaking students, are sensitive to cultural differences and would therefore not construct them as culturally deficient or deprived. Although that may be true, the continued uncritical use of needs analysis in EAP, both the term and the process, must be problematized and balanced with analysis that makes room for student dissent and activism.

RIGHTS ANALYSIS

To conceptualize a more active role for students in shaping the target situation and to focus attention on the politics of education, I use *rights analysis* (Benesch 1999a), discussed in chapters 3 and 4. Considering *rights* in addition to *needs, wants, lacks,* and other terms found in the needs analysis literature (Hutchinson & Waters, 1987) shifts attention from institutional requirements to possibilities for student engagement and change. It highlights authority, control, participation, and resistance, issues not usually discussed in relation to target situations. Yet, rights are neither entitlements nor a fixed set of demands. Rather, they are a framework for understanding and responding to power relations. Rights analysis is a theoretical tool for EAP teachers and students to consider possible responses to unfavorable social, institutional, and classroom conditions. Some questions that might be posed are: What are the rules governing this situation? Who formulated those rules? How do the participants respond to them? What are the forms of resistance? Where are the areas of negotiation? (Benesch, 1999a).

Taking rights into account, however, does not exclude attention to needs. Needs analysis and rights analysis are in a dialectical relationship. The first represents stability and accommodation; the second represents resistance and change. In critical EAP, both requirements and dissent are taken into account. Needs analysis addresses target situation demands, yet rights analysis allows for the possibility of challenging and transforming unreasonable and inequitable arrangements. The linked psychology/EAP writing class described in this chapter is an example of both needs and rights analysis, fulfilling target requirements while experimenting with ways to modify them. It also theorizes rights as a space where alternatives to the status quo might be shaped, both inside academic institutions and in other areas of students' present and future lives. It is a way for students to question what is usually taken for granted.

Rights analysis is informed by Foucault's concept of power, the notion that power is multiple and pervasive, and that power and resistance co-exist. It is a way to study "the specificity of mechanisms of power" (Foucault, 1980, p. 145) or the "procedures of power" (p. 148), how it works technically in local settings. It also entails studying resistance "right at the point where relations of power are exercised" (p. 142).

PROBLEMATIZING RIGHTS

The use of *rights*, while justifiable as a counterhegemonic response to *needs*, nonetheless, raises a concern related to the patriarchal model of democracy discussed in chapter 3. That is, if rights are associated with the model of democracy formulated by Greek philosophers, who viewed them as the exclusive domain of men, are they the appropriate tool for discovering possibilities for dissent by all students in a contemporary university? Perhaps a term unburdened by masculinist assumptions would be more appropriate, such as *possibilities* (Simon, 1992) or *hope*. Another problem with *rights*, as mentioned before, is its association with pre-established political demands or entitlements, such as the right to organize or the right to free speech.

Despite these problems, I choose to retain *rights* simply because *needs* requires a more overtly political complement than either *possibilities* or *hope* can provide. Although those terms have the advantage of implying openness to change without a priori expectations, they lack the sense of organized resistance. Rights, on the other hand, a historically contested term with connotations of pre-existing prerogatives, nonetheless highlights the politics of critical EAP. However, I emphasize that rights are not pre-established but must be discovered in each setting. The possibilities for students to organize for change depend on the relationship between power and resistance in that particular situation. Critical EAP does not assume that students are necessarily entitled to a set of rights worked out on their behalf that they may call on as enfranchised members of a pre-existing community with shared goals. Rather, the aim of rights analysis is to discover what is possible, desirable, and beneficial at a certain moment with a particular group of students.

THE TARGET AS A SITE OF STRUGGLE

The rights analysis discussed in this chapter explores how power was exercised by the institution, the psychology professor, the EAP students, and me, and how it was resisted and negotiated. The setting was a psychology course, taught by Professor Bell, with 43 students, 20 of whom were also enrolled in my EAP writing course. The psychology class met 3 hours a week, a 2-hour session on Mondays and a 1-hour session on Wednesdays, most of which I attended. The EAP class met right after. Professor Bell and I each received 1 hour of released time to meet weekly to discuss ways to enhance the link between our courses and to exchange thoughts about student progress.[11]

Establishing Procedures and Rules on the First Day

At the beginning of the first psychology class meeting, Bell distributed a course outline, half of which described rules regarding attendance, lateness, absence from exams, and grades. For example: "There are no makeup exams in the course. Absence from an exam will result in a failing grade." The other half of the outline included the topics to be covered. No reading assignments were included, although the title of the textbook was listed.

Bell told students that there would be three multiple-choice exams, each covering different chapters. He then made the following observation: "I don't go back over previous material, so as soon as you take the exam, you'll forget the material." Next, he described a study of how much material is retained by college students from the time they are tested on it to the time they leave school and over subsequent years. On the board, he drew a graph demonstrating a steady drop in retention from right after the time a test is taken to a few years later when nothing is retained.

Perhaps in response to the graph's dramatic illustration of how steadily academic material is forgotten, one student asked, "Don't the tests depend on how good your memory is?" Bell answered, "The more you understand the concepts, the better you remember the details. I can't think of any class where memory isn't important. Psychology is so big, it's impossible for anyone to be an expert in all 350 subfields." The same student replied, "Nobody's memory is that good," suggesting concern about the complete reliance on memorization of the testing and grading procedures. Rather than responding to this concern, Bell encouraged the students to ask questions whenever they liked. He then began a lecture based on chapter 1 of the textbook about the subfields of psychology. He spoke clearly and gave alternative expressions for terms that might be unfamiliar. He did not write on the board or pause for questions.

Student Resistance: Complaints and Written Feedback

During the first EAP class meeting, students filled out demographic questionnaires, carried out paired interviews, discussed their goals, and

---

[11]This linked course was funded in part by The City University of New York's 1997 Campus-Based Innovative English as a Second Language Programs.

wrote about their prior writing experiences in L1 and L2. These activities were intended to begin the community-building process. After explaining the relationship between the linked courses, I mentioned that I would ask Professor Bell to write on the board during future lectures to facilitate note-taking.

During the second EAP class meeting, a few students asked me to make other requests to Bell. One commented that because the syllabus did not contain reading assignments, he would not be able to prepare for upcoming lectures. Others concurred, pointing out that they were lost listening to lectures when they had not had a chance to preview material, expressing a wish for information about which textbook pages to read in advance.

Rather than continuing to act as intermediary between the students and Bell, I made a writing assignment in the EAP class whose purpose was to formalize some of the concerns students were voicing about the lectures and how they related to the textbook chapters. The assignment was to write any suggestions they had for Bell for ways to change the psychology class. The written responses ranged from apparent acceptance of the status quo to apologetic suggestions to emphatic proposals for adjustments to the current conditions. For example, one female student expressed her complete satisfaction with the class due to the changes already made:

> I believe that the way our psychology professor is teaching right now, with board-writing, reviewing and slow explanations is real good. I feel I can follow the lessons and he is very patient if I ask about a word I don't understand. So right now, after the improvements that are already done, I do not know of any changes he could do to make it easier for me.

Another female student was more tentative in her acceptance of the status quo. However, she believed the responsibility for making sense of the lecture and textbook material rested solely with her:

> I think I'm OK with the lecture. I just have to put more efforts into reading and understanding the contents myself.

Two male students expressed overall satisfaction with the class, but each offered suggestions for improvement:

> Actually I'm almost satisfied with the lectures. The only thing I'd like to change is a hometask. It would be much more simpler if he would give us a concrete homework after each class, so we know what is gonna be on the next lesson and can do both: Repeat previous material and be prepared for the next one.

> In general I really like Prof. B's teaching style. Also I like the adjustments he made from our previous suggestions. The only thing that I would like to suggest is if he could start the class by entertaining questions from the previous

lesson because sometimes after reviewing my notes and the book, some questions pop out that I was not aware of before and during the class.

Another male student described his loss of concentration after an hour of listening to a 2-hour lecture. His proposal calls for prior exposure to material as preparation for nonstop lecturing:

> Usually I don't have problems understanding what he explains. While I am in class, after an hour, suddenly something else (not related to this class) comes to my mind for 3–5 minutes then I lose track. Then when I pay attention, I can't figure out what he's talking about. I think if he could tell us the things that he will cover at the following lecture, then we could read those things before class and we would have a better idea about what's going on in the class.

Two female students who had been struggling with the new and abstract lecture material asked for more concrete examples and more writing on the board:

> I wish Dr. B. would give us more simple examples. Like true life story.

> I wish Prof. B. would write down the words on the board.

Victor's Response: Resistance and Compliance

One written proposal combined acceptance of certain features of Bell's class with suggestions for modification. The student, Victor, takes responsibility for studying and understanding material on his own, but also gives several thoughtful proposals for ways to improve the class. He begins his feedback by pointing out that the class is challenging for a first-year student, especially one who has never studied psychology before. Victor goes on to acknowledge his duty as a student to make sense of the material. However, he then suggests making time for student discussion and questions. Finally, he proposes using class time to go over the textbook rather than simply assigning pages to be read at home. Victor suggested this, I believe, not to avoid homework but to have the opportunity to discuss difficult passages with Professor Bell, as we had done in the EAP class:

> I am a freshman and this is my first psychology class. I get the lessons and understand most of them. The rest I have to study and understand by myself. We have a good system going on, but I think we can upgrade this, like, for example, the time. I think that our two hours on Monday can be modified. The first hour he could use for his lecture. He can even make it an hour and a half; the second part I think we could use as a class discussion type of thing with everybody giving examples and asking relevant questions. He could also do this with the Wednesday class even though it's only an hour, or we could use the time to go over the book together instead of making us read them at home.

Up to this point, Victor's tone is polite, yet unapologetic. His suggestions are made in a friendly and collegial manner. However, a shift in tone occurs in the next two sentences where he begins to backpedal, perhaps signaling that he thinks he has gone too far in questioning professorial authority by suggesting a modification in the use of class time: "My opinion I think will take too much time and we would be behind in our schedule." Then, he closes even more modestly with a self-effacing request to simply slow down for the EAP students: "So if he could not do these he could at least slow down a little bit for us foreign students."

Victor's responses, like those of students who might have been reluctant to propose changes they would have welcomed, can be seen as examples of self-surveillance (a Foucauldian construct referring to the internalization of institutional regulations) (Bartky, 1988). Even before Bell rejects his suggestions, Victor downplays them "thus exercising this surveillance over and against himself" (Foucault, 1980, p. 155) without the need for external control. Victor does not wait to be told that his proposals violate the current regime; he anticipates their rejection by dismissing them himself and retreating to the subordinate and outsider's position of "foreign student".[12]

However, self-surveillance is not the sole way to understand Victor's shifting stance. The proposal can also be read as an example of the tension between student compliance and resistance. He and other students showed that they imagined alternatives to the status quo, expressing their concerns about the psychology class first verbally and informally and then in writing, in fulfillment of my assignment. They responded to institutional and professorial authority and rituals with alternative ways to structure classroom time and talk. Yet, Victor's abandonment of his own suggestions signals either a fear of retribution or nervousness about his position in the classroom hierarchy: Who am I, a mere foreign student, he seems to be saying, to propose such changes? The uneasy relationship between teacher power and student resistance permeates his written response.

Bell's reaction to the students' proposals reveals how accurate Victor had been in anticipating the response. After reading all the suggestions, during one of our weekly meetings, Bell asked me to communicate the following remarks to the EAP class in which he reiterates the current regime of permitting questions without making any structural changes. It is interesting to note that he chose not to address the students directly, thus maintaining his distance, as they had done in writing about him in the third person in their proposals. Yet, that distance may have been a function of my continued role as go-between, despite my efforts to bring about a more direct exchange between Bell and the students:

---

[12]Though Victor uses the term *foreign student*, his family had emigrated from the Philippines, where he had completed high school, the previous year. They had no plans to return to that country.

> I have no problems with students asking questions before the class. This thing about questions: I could have a period for that, but questions are always OK. Tell them they can ask questions anytime. As far as what's going on in the next lecture, I can try. Tell them if I forget they can remind me, or ask me, "What's going on in the next lecture?" "Would you mind telling us what the next lecture will be on?" If anyone wants to ask me, "Is there something from real life or human beings?", that's OK. Just remind me with a question.

These comments made it clear that the students' proposals for setting aside time for discussion of lecture and textbook material would not be incorporated. Instead, Bell re-established the policy of permitting students to ask questions before, during, and after lectures. However, as they began to take the offer to ask questions seriously, Bell ran into a problem covering the material appearing on upcoming exams, revealing a conflict between coverage and dialogue.

COVERAGE AS CONTROL

The psychology course was an introductory survey designed, according to Bell, to offer "a general appreciation of basic concepts that exist in the field of psychology . . . some appreciation of the techniques that are used . . . and some understanding of competing theories that explain different observations" (Bell, personal communication, May 1997). For the 16-week semester during which my EAP course was linked to his psychology course, Bell had chosen nine topics to cover: introduction and research methodology; learning and intelligence; tests and measurement; memory and cognition; motivation; emotion and stress; theories of personality; abnormal psychology; and therapy. Because each multiple-choice test was based on three of these topics, there was a compulsion to get through a certain amount of material each week. Therefore, a conflict between coverage and dialogue emerged. The more questions the students asked during lectures, the less material could be presented, delaying the upcoming exam and causing a backup for subsequent exams.

In an interview with Bell at the end of the semester, I explored the tension between coverage and participation, first by asking about the role of student questions. He told me:

> I enjoy answering their questions and I like it when they ask questions because it shows that they're thinking about what we're doing and they're *actively* involved in the lecture. They're putting something of themselves into it. So it shows they're paying attention, that they're active participants in the learning. And I think asking and getting answers to questions promotes more interest. I always encourage it. And I think it helps other people learn too. Cause very often several people might be thinking the same thing.

Next, I asked how he dealt with having to cover material when students wanted to ask questions. He answered:

> I try to keep the time frame in mind as best I can so I allow for as much of that as I can, keeping in mind that I want to cover a certain amount of material. So, it's true I have to even curtail what *I'm* gonna say sometimes. I want to add something also that I can't because there's not enough time to do it. It's annoying.

Bell continued by offering a description of ways coverage controls both student and teacher talk. These comments highlight the conflict between encouraging participation and moving on to cover new material, whether or not students have understood previous concepts:

> I really think questions from the students should . . . I love to answer every single one of them and let it go on until there's no more questions. And I'd like to be able to say what I want to say. I just don't feel like I'm doing enough. But I have a time constraint and I can't do it. Things come up that you don't even expect. Maybe something took longer because maybe there were more questions here. So, it's hard to figure out over the term of the course because a topic may have taken way longer than . . . now I have to take it from someplace else. The thing that I'm most interested in, I have to do the least with . . . This thing with abnormal psych and I could go on, you know, I didn't cover. I didn't go into the detail that I normally do and I had to rush over it. There wasn't enough time. But why wasn't there enough time? I don't even know what happened this semester. I can't even figure it out.

I suggested to him that the increased participation of EAP students may have taken up time he would have had to cover material had they not been asking questions. He agreed that their questions may have led him to feel more rushed in the Psychology 100 section linked with the EAP course than in the other section he taught that semester. Yet, he also offered that the students in the section with the linked EAP class were more engaged:

> There were definitely, definitely more questions. Way more interest in this class. It was a totally different atmosphere, in a positive direction. People enjoyed being with each other . . . They were comfortable in the class. They were comfortable asking questions; they looked happier; there was more smiling; there was more conversation. When I walked into the class, they'd be talking to each other. I liked it better. It was more comfortable for me. I enjoyed coming to this class because of it. . . . It was very good, very good.

So, although Bell was more comfortable in the class where students participated, he was simultaneously worried that he would not be able to cover as much as he needed to prepare students for the upcoming test.

The overriding contradiction, however, is that Bell had acknowledged on the first day the course met that the pedagogy was bankrupt: The students would be required to memorize information in order to be tested, but they would soon forget the material. So, why continue with this way of teaching? Why, despite the preponderance of evidence pointing to the relationship between talking, writing, and learning (Hirsch, 1988; Mayher, Lester, & Pradl, 1983; Smoke, 1994, 1998; Zamel, 1995), does coverage of certain amounts of material, through lecturing and testing, continue to dominate college teaching worldwide?

From a political perspective, it may be that lecturing persists because it is a means of institutional and cultural control over students and teachers alike. If, in each of their courses, students must memorize large amounts of standardized textbook information, there is less chance for them to challenge the status quo. They are kept so busy listening to lectures, taking notes, reading textbooks, memorizing definitions, and taking tests that they have little time to occupy themselves with larger questions: How does education relate to my everyday life? Who decided that this is the knowledge I should learn? Where did this information come from?

For their part, teachers are so consumed with covering material that they have little time to get to know the students, listen to their questions, invite them to write about and discuss course material, and encourage them to reflect on the education they are receiving. The requirement to cover rather than promote dialogue can be an alienating experience for students and teachers alike.

NEEDS AND RIGHTS ANALYSES
IN THE LINKED COURSE

Bell lectured; the students were expected to listen and take notes. In addition, students were required to read chapters in the assigned textbook related to the lecture material. That is, needs analysis revealed that the EAP class should focus on listening, note-taking, textbook reading, and test-taking skills. Indeed, substantial time was devoted to these activities in the linked EAP class that met after the lecture class. For example, different students would volunteer to summarize psychology lectures for homework. During the following EAP class, those summaries would be compared with others' lecture notes. Students would then try to clarify their notes through discussion and by consulting the textbook. An activity related to the three exams was for groups of students to write multiple-choice questions and answers and test each other in preparation for upcoming exam.

In addition, there were activities designed to supplement the lecture content. For example, after a film documenting Milgram's landmark study of obedience was shown in the psychology class, I asked students to write about a time when they had to choose whether or not to obey a person in authority, an assignment I had made several years earlier yielding interesting essays (Benesch, 1988). This and similar writing assignments aimed to concretize the material by bringing it into the personal realm. Because they helped to support the material offered in the lecture class, these assignments fall under the needs-analysis rubric.

Rights analysis, on the other hand, revealed the dynamics between institutional and professorial authority and student resistance to rules and regulations. Attending psychology lectures with the students permitted me to observe their reactions to the class, listen to their questions, and observe their interaction with each other. As participant observer, I took notes on both the lectures and what I observed (I also recorded the lectures). In the EAP class, I noted students' concerns about the difficulty of listening for long periods of time, the challenge of hearing new words but not seeing them written on the board, and the frustration of trying to understand abstract definitions.

After it became clear that no structural modifications in the lecture class would be made in response to students' proposals and that questions were the sole instrument of overt student participation, we spent time in the EAP class working on ways to ask questions. Also, I suggested that EAP students sit together in the first two rows of the lecture class so that they could help each other with questions, creating a more participatory climate. For example, during a lecture on primary and secondary reinforcers in behaviorism, Bell defined secondary reinforcers as "larger things we will work for that are learned; we learn to want them" and he offered money as an example. Marie, a Haitian student asked, "Could it also be a prize? Like if you do a science project and you get a *ruban.*" Not understanding *ruban,* Bell asked "A what?" Other students translated the word for Bell as ribbon. This type of attention to each others' questions and supportive interaction between EAP students was noted by Bell during our final interview: "They were into it, almost enjoying each other's asking questions. They kind of all got into it. One person asked a question and they'd all be behind it, be participating somehow in this person asking a question."

QUESTIONS: CONFLICT BETWEEN
COVERAGE AND COMPREHENSION

As the previous example shows, questions functioned as a way to get Bell to offer examples and clarification of the concepts he defined. At times, they also enabled students to curtail the introduction of new material when previous concepts had not been fully understood. Written feedback from Ali, a student who rarely asked questions, suggests that questions may, in part, have functioned in this way:

> I really think that in order to make it easier for me to understand the lecture, I need some time to capture the information. I think the questions give me time to do that. When people ask some questions, I take my rest.

For example, during the first lecture on abnormal psychology toward the end of the semester, Bell quickly went through much new material, as if he were working his way down a list, spending no time elaborating. He seemed to be covering topics so they could be included on the final exam. In response to this speeded-up lecturing, students jumped in with questions. Bell introduced a new topic in the lecture, anxiety disorders, in the following way:

> Anxiety disorders are one type of emotional disorder. They used to be called neuroses. One is generalized anxiety disorder. It's someone who worries a lot and seeks reassurance from other people. They have trouble sleeping, they sweat, they have stomach problems. They always feel tense.

As Bell was about to go on to the next anxiety disorder on the list without elaborating the first, one student asked, "Is that the same as seeking approval?" Bell answered, "No. They worry." He then went on to the next disorder with no further clarification or response to the student's question:

> With panic disorders there's a sudden wave of anxiety. The heart rate is elevated, there's tingling, heat, and sweating.

Another student jumped in, "Are they just thinking this or is it really happening?" And before Bell could reply, another asked, "If you feel faint, how am I going to convince you that you don't feel faint?" After answering the first of these questions and ignoring the second, perhaps being reluctant to take time to ask the student to explain its meaning, Bell moved on to the next anxiety disorder, phobias:

> It's an irrational fear of something. You'd do anything to avoid it. Agoraphobia is the fear of open or unfamiliar places. It's a fear of going to places far from home, a fear of leaving home. It's common among people who have panic disorders.

A student then asked, before Bell could go on to the next subject, "Are they afraid of the crowds or of the place?" After answering this question, Bell signaled to the students that he no longer wanted to elaborate on the short definitions he was giving because of time constraints: "There's lots I could tell you about this stuff, but there isn't enough time."

The struggle between Bell and the students over how much time to spend on topics was ongoing. When students needed time to process material, they asked questions. When Bell wanted to move quickly through the lecture, he either ignored their questions or stopped allowing questions, as in the previous example. That is, even though Bell had told the class that they could ask questions whenever they liked, he violated his own policy when the pressure to cover material for an upcoming test was mounting.

Although students' attempts to elicit further clarification and elaboration from Bell seemed genuine, there were times when questions may have been used as a way to take a break from listening. This is not to say that these questions were mere interruptions, but rather, that they may have given students more control over how much material could be presented during a 1- or 2-hour lecture.

THE ROLE OF A CRITICAL EAP TEACHER

Emerging from rights analysis is the issue of the critical EAP teacher's role. As the EAP teacher observing the struggle between the content teacher and students over the speed of lecture delivery and classroom talk, I was in a position of conflict: Do I simply help students absorb as much information as possible or do I encourage them to ask questions to increase their understanding and provide a more interactive atmosphere in the linked course? That is, do I focus mainly on target needs or on students' expressed desire to intervene in the process through more active participation? I found myself shuttling back and forth between the two, honoring the stable and predictable routines of the lecture class while encouraging the interaction and dialogue students had asked for in their written proposals to allow them to make sense of new material.

What was my influence on the dynamics in the lecture class? Was I imposing a "confrontational stance towards current discourse practices" (p. 231), a concern raised by Dudley-Evans and St. John (1998) about critical approaches to EAP? Or, was I simply encouraging students to channel the frustration they were already feeling during the first psychology lecture when a flood of new words was put into circulation with no board-writing and limited explanation. That frustration intensified before exams when new definitions were put forth with no elaboration and little connection to previous concepts or student experience, as the example from the abnormal psychology lecture showed.

I would claim that the conflict between coverage and dialogue was hidden just below the surface and my role as a critical EAP teacher was to expose it. The conflict resided in academic power arrangements founded on transmission and testing, a failed pedagogy of memorization and forgetting (Cummins & Sayers, 1995; Hutchinson & Waters, 1987; Lave, 1997; Moll, 1989) . Students were expected to accept these conditions, but instead, they resisted in a variety of ways: Some came late to the lecture class; some talked to each other; some complained. Rather than continuing to observe these behaviors, painful and futile attempts to redress the power imbalance and achieve greater understanding, I chose to help students channel their resistance into proposals and actions to improve conditions. The result was a more active and participatory psychology class in which EAP students received a higher mean grade (2.3050) than the other students (2.1391) although the difference between the mean grades failed to reach statistical significance.

What are the long-term results of rights analysis? Is there a way to measure the lasting effects of encouraging students to turn their complaints into proposals and to intervene by asking questions? Auerbach and McGrail (1991) grapple with the question of outcomes in critical pedagogy and whether each lesson or course must lead to observable changes in order to fulfill its critical claims. They conclude that "change takes many forms, both inside and outside the classroom, and may not be packaged in discrete actions but rather in the gradual, cumulative building of confidence, validation of experience, and change in perspective" (p. 105). Although it may take years for students to engage in actions outside the classroom, critical pedagogy meanwhile allows for "changing social relations within the classroom, the critical examination of day-to-day reality, and the development of language and literacy" (p. 105).

The active participation of EAP students changed the dynamics in Bell's class, leading him to comment that there was "a totally different atmosphere, in a positive direction." It was a class in which he felt more comfortable than in classes where students were less engaged. That does not mean that Bell's pedagogy changed as a result of this experience. However, this was not the goal of critical EAP. Rather, it was to engage students in a semester-long process of simultaneously learning the material and challenging the lecture style, to get more out of it and to struggle against it. Formalizing their resistance was the critical work. It may encourage them to challenge other unfavorable situations inside and outside of classrooms.

SUMMARY

The rights analysis I carried out in the EAP/psychology linked course revealed that target requirements, pedagogy, and rules were sites of struggle. After the rules were established, students resisted certain features of the target, offering suggestions for ways to make it a more hospitable environment for learning. The main area of struggle was over how time should be spent. Bell felt compelled to cover a certain amount of material; students were overwhelmed by the number of new concepts introduced during each lecture. Bell was interested in their questions but faced the demands of multiple-choice testing requiring memorization of unconnected facts.

Dialogic teaching is an ideal not easily achieved when the tradition of lecturing about discrete bits of information to be covered on a test prevails. Even in content courses where coverage of a certain amount of material is not the goal, transforming practice is difficult. This challenge is taken up in the next chapter.

Chapter 8

A Negotiated Assignment: Possibilities and Challenges

The examples of critical EAP in previous chapters were linked to undergraduate general education courses whose curricula followed departmental guidelines and the content teacher's chosen textbook. Although in two of those cases, I met with the content teacher before the semester began to discuss reading and writing assignments, the pedagogy and syllabi of the content course were not negotiated. The expectation was that the EAP class would facilitate student understanding of concepts introduced in the content class. This arrangement constructed EAP as a service course, although in the examples I show how that positioning can be challenged by the EAP teacher through alternative curricular choices and mediation of student resistance to unfavorable conditions.

The EAP courses described in this chapter, offered through the College of Staten Island Freshman Workshop Program (FWP), were not linked to lecture courses nor was the content-course syllabus predetermined. Rather, the FWP had been set up to facilitate curricular and pedagogical negotiation and collaboration across the curriculum (Benesch, 1988; Ortiz, 1996). FWP's deliberate divergence from the usual conventions of coverage and teacher-dominated talk elevates EAP from a subordinate role in the content/language relationship to an equal partner. FWP faculty collaborate with each other and with students about teaching and materials to provide an intellectually engaging experience. Central to the pedagogy is allowing the courses to be guided by the pace of student engagement and understanding. That is, the curriculum is cocreated by teachers and students as the course progresses, taking students' questions and difficulties into account.

The negotiated assignment in one linked course discussed in this chapter highlights alternatives to the traditional role of EAP as a support to preestablished aims and procedures of content courses. Yet, it also points to the challenges of breaking through the content-coverage tradition, even when those types of demands are not institutionally or programmatically mandated, as does the second example from another linked course.

THE CONTEXT

In 1970, the City University of New York (CUNY) Board of Higher Education voted in a policy of open admissions, which guaranteed that every New York City high school graduate would be admitted to one of the CUNY colleges. This new policy allowed students into the university who had previously been shut out because their high school averages were below a designated cutoff or because they were in the bottom half of their graduating class. The new policy also guaranteed transfer from 2-year to 4-year colleges. The student population of CUNY rose from 27,000 in 1968 to 200,000 in 1998. Colleges developed innovative programs to accommodate the new students and open admissions conferences were held in which ideas about teaching nontraditional students were shared. It was a time of hope and innovation.

English department faculty at the College of Staten Island, then a community college, initiated several programs to accommodate open admissions students, including the Freshman Workshop Program (FWP), which offered blocks of writing, reading, and content courses. When I was appointed to the college in 1985, the program had been institutionalized following extensive piloting and refinements. The FWP's philosophy was that learning and metacognitive awareness, not coverage, would be the overriding concern: ". . . there is no intent or compulsion to 'cover' any predetermined amount of material . . . The concentration of teacher and student is more on developing the students' awareness of their learning processes and of what being a student requires—questioning, active involvement with intellectual material, a critical stance—rather than a predetermined content" (R. Ortiz, personal communication, 1986).

Those who chose to teach in the program took a 1-semester course, the Developmental Education Study Group, in which the relationship between teaching, learning, and language was addressed through exercises, shared assignments, and readings. Along with the study group, participating faculty were given 1 hour of released time for weekly meetings to formulate assignments, discuss student progress, and exchange feedback. Content and language faculty determined collaboratively how to handle the links between their courses, with the understanding that "no course should sacrifice its goals to meet the needs of the others" (Ortiz, 1997, p. 3).

Ortiz (1996) has observed that faculty in linked courses coordinate their instruction in various ways: thematically, where a single theme, or set of themes, is shared by the three instructors; methodologically, where teaching techniques, such as peer group work, are the common bond; and procedurally, where the same questions are used in each class as "entry into different content" (p. 6). An example of a thematic link is the unit on obedience discussed in Benesch (1988) in which a film about Stanley Milgram's experiment was screened in the psychology class and used as the basis of a writing assignment in the EAP class with students writing about a time that they had to choose whether or not to obey. Ortiz (1996) cites several examples of methodological links, a common one being the use of mapping in the content and language classes to allow students to visualize abstract material. One example of a procedural link is the use of documents in a history/English link in which students were asked to attend to details as a way to understand both primary sources and literary texts. Whatever faculty choose as their way of coordinating instruction, the content course is not the nucleus around which the reading and writing courses revolve. Rather, the equal importance of all three is a precept of the FWP, making this program different from the traditional arrangement of EAP as the support or service to content courses.

Designed for students who had failed the CUNY freshman skills tests on entry, the FWP has never offered academic credit toward a degree but rather elective credit,[13] giving participating faculty flexibility in what they offer free of the constraints of an introductory survey course with its prescribed content. However, there are also disadvantages to FWP's positioning as a remedial (and ESL) program, rather than a mainstreamed one. These disadvantages surfaced in the mid-1990s when the political climate shifted the university's commitment away from open-admissions students toward transfer and upper-division students, along with continued cuts in public funding for higher education, making certain features of the FWP vulnerable to elimination. First, the study group was dismantled and then released time for weekly meetings was removed. These changes diminished opportunities for collaboration, although those who had participated in the study group in previous semesters strived to convey that spirit to newly participating faculty who had not. In addition, elective credits were removed from the reading and writing courses, making them into noncredit courses, but not from the content courses. This change led to a symbolically more hierarchical arrangement of content at the top and language as its support. Despite the changes, the FWP has endured, thanks in large part to the persistence of committed faculty in the English Department as well as the college's administration.

The first example in this chapter is from a block of three linked courses: ESL reading, ESL writing, and introduction to social science, taught in

---

[13]Each degree program, such as computer science or psychology, requires a specific number of credits. However, the required courses for the degree, including basic and distribution requirements, may not add up to a sufficient number of credits needed to qualify for an associate's or bachelor's diploma. So, students are allowed to take elective credits, offerings outside their degree programs, to fulfill the total for graduation.

spring 1992, before modifications were made to the FWP. It details an assignment negotiated by students and the three teachers, showing what issues were raised when the syllabus was not fixed but instead was guided, at least in part, by students' personal and social concerns. It demonstrates both the positive and negative outcomes of an experiment in critical EAP in which students' responses to course material were allowed to guide the pace of teaching. The example is not intended to illustrate a particular method of critical teaching but, rather, the challenges and benefits of grounding instruction in students' experience. It demonstrates the difficulty of bringing about more dialogic teaching even in a setting conducive to experimentation and collaboration, and shows that the tradition of lecturing and coverage is not easily supplanted.

WHAT CONFUSES YOU ABOUT U.S. SOCIETY?
A NEGOTIATED ASSIGNMENT

The ESL reading, ESL writing, and social science teacher, all full-time tenured professors, collaborated before the semester began on how to coordinate instruction, including which texts to assign. Professor Carroll, a historian who taught the social science class, believed that everything was rooted in the economy. He therefore wanted to focus his course on economic theory and history and proposed assigning Heilbroner's (1992) *The Making of Economic Society* in his class. Having successfully taught historical fiction and wanting to focus on American social history, the reading teacher, Professor Martin, chose Doctorow's (1974) *Ragtime* for the EAP reading class. I chose Mathabane's (1989) *Kaffir Boy in America* for the EAP writing class, as a trigger for writing assignments about social problems in U.S. society, to orient students to the writing assessment test they would retake at the end of the semester, an argumentative essay on a social issue.

In addition to consulting about our texts, the three teachers decided to launch the semester with a question that might figure into work in all three classes: What confuses you about U.S. society? The idea was to elicit issues and concerns the students wanted to address and to follow up with related reading and writing assignments. We did not plan to structure the entire semester around students' responses to that question, but wanted to at least begin that way. Despite the apparent simplicity of this question, however, it required mediation, an observation that we found applied also to other assignments throughout the semester. That is, because the FWP is not primarily concerned with content mastery but more fundamentally with how students make sense, or not, of academic material, the teachers are encouraged to be guided by student feedback, including confusion and tentativeness as well as interest, enthusiasm, and curiosity. This focus, though, was more easily accepted by the language teachers who are generally more accustomed to dealing with learning processes than content teachers, who are used to covering material with perhaps less direct attention to learning itself. The conflict between learning and coverage was apparent in these linked courses as it was in the others discussed in previous chapters. As Ortiz (1996) observes, "While English teachers can use the materials of the discipline course with which they are linked, they cannot move through them as quickly as the discipline course may demand" (p. 7).

When Carroll posed the question, "What confuses you about U.S. society?" on the first day his class met, many of the students responded with silence, perhaps unsure of what he was seeking. Even his request to do free writing about the topic was fulfilled by only half the class. Had he been teaching an unlinked course, he might have reverted to the traditional lecturing mode, being discouraged by the students' reserve. However, the link provided opportunities to pursue the question rather than abandoning it. During the faculty meeting following the class where Carroll had posed the question, we decided that I, as the writing teacher, should make it into a writing assignment, including brainstorming, listing, and composing.

At the beginning of the next writing class meeting, I asked the students why they had had trouble responding to Carroll's question. One student replied, "Everything is confusing. I am living so it's difficult to write about it. I have no time to observe and see, no time think about it. So I don't know what to write." Another said, "I don't understand the question." And a third helpfully offered, "We need to talk about it." In the ensuing discussion, the question was clarified. Brainstorming encouraged students to suggest possible topics, even those who had initially thought they had nothing to write about. The class ended with free writing on a chosen topic. At home, students wrote drafts using the in-class discussion and writing to guide them. During the following writing class meeting, they read the drafts to each other in small groups. They then chose excerpts from their drafts, in consultation with peer group members, to share with the whole group. The following are excerpts from those drafts:

Why so beautiful and rich New York City has so many homeless?

This year the [subway] token rate is $1.25. I have been taking the train to school everyday. Many people are mad because they pay the increased fare but the government isn't providing them benefit, such as more trains at rush hour.

Before I came to the U.S. I thought that U.S. is a very advanced country. But when I look around NY city, the famous business city, it isn't so advanced, like the subway. And I think that U.S. put most of their money and technology into the military.

My son goes to second grade in public school and the system confuses me because it is not hard work.

I'm against the help the government gives to people that really can get a job. It should only be for older people.

People pay money, about five to ten dollars before crossing a bridge. If you don't have money, you can't cross from one island to the other.

Sometimes I just couldn't figure out for which products do you have to pay tax or don't . . . Also by the end of each year you must prepare tax return form. I don't understand why if you are making "big money" you have to pay higher tax.

USA is spending so much money for war and arms. If they use only one tenth money from the arms budget, then all the people can live nicely.

I was surprised that the responses related mainly to money, both personal finances and social spending, having anticipated that issues such as racism and crime would be the primary concerns. The students may have been guided in part by the economic focus of the social science class. Yet their answers seemed to indicate that for these immigrants with multiple financial burdens of education, transportation, housing, child rearing, and paying taxes, economic issues were the area of greatest confusion. When the three teachers got together to read the papers, Professor Carroll came up with an interesting idea: Because many of the students were curious about U.S. spending priorities, we would ask them to research the allocation of different items in the federal, state, and city budgets and then write about whether they thought adjustments should be made in spending.

During the meeting, to prepare for this assignment, Carroll began to derive categories from the students' papers: transportation, education, the military, and so on. Although Professor Martin and I agreed that the students' drafts should be the basis for further research, we wondered if they would see the connection between what they had written and this next assignment, especially if they had not come up with the categories themselves. We decided that I should give back the papers during the following writing class meeting and propose a series of activities designed to put the students in charge of the research.

During the EAP writing class, I returned the students' drafts and asked them to underline the most important sentences in their compositions. I then asked them to write those sentences on the board, and as a class, to come up with a category for each sentence, ending up with a list of topics. Next, they formed research groups, based on one of the topics. There were six groups, each of which was focused on one of the topics they had identified: education, foreign aid, NASA, defense, Environmental Protection Agency, or transportation. In the groups, they wrote what they already knew about the topic followed by research questions detailing what they wanted to find out. For example, the foreign aid group wrote the following questions: What is the federal budget for foreign aid? Who gets the money? Who decides how much to give out? What requirements do those countries have to have in order to receive foreign aid? Does the U.S. get the money back? How does the money get there? What does the U.S. gain from giving them foreign aid? What do these countries use the money for?

The next part of the assignment was carried out under Carroll's supervision. Combining library research and consultation with him, the students found answers to their questions and wrote them in their research journals. The data collection was collaborative, but Carroll wanted the students to write their final papers individually so that he could give them each a separate grade. His assignment was to write a two-page paper. The first page was to include answers to five of the original research questions, devoting a paragraph to each one. The second page was to be an argument for more or less government spending on the group's topic. After students had written their individual papers, the groups got back together to develop a debate, with half the group members arguing for more spending on their budget category and the other arguing for less. The debates were held in two content-class meetings with whole-class discussion following each debate.

During the period the students were working on their individual papers and organizing their debates, the three teachers discussed the progress of the series of assignments. One of the more predictable concerns was that the least-skilled students were copying data directly from the articles and books they found in the library. I worked with those students in their groups and individually to make sense of the material and translate it into prose that revealed their understanding, however tentative. One advantage of this particular research assignment was that it was grounded in questions the students had posed. Therefore, even when they struggled with the reading and writing, the purpose of the work was clear.

Another ongoing concern for Carroll was how to encourage students to continue when they seemed reluctant to follow through with their assignments. He did not assume that they were obstinately refusing to work but was surprised at their periodic inability to go on ("I thought that assignment was clear"). These roadblocks, so familiar to language teachers, who do not expect lessons to go smoothly and are used to relying on student confusion to guide them, discouraged Professor Carroll who, during one of our meetings, observed with some dismay that all assignments required so much coaching. His discouragement seemed to stem from the habit of letting the curriculum guide the pace of presentation rather than students' understanding of the material. As he said, during our final discussion about the budget assignments: "I got restless. I like to work at an even pace throughout the semester. The group work slows it down."

Carroll's comments about pace and teacher boredom raise important questions about what happens when the focus of instruction is not a predetermined syllabus but the students' questions and their pace of work when researching answers to those questions. The FWP was set up to help open admissions students simultaneously learn new material and develop metacognitive skills that might carry over into other academic classes. It encourages faculty to stay with activities, not race from chapter to chapter in a textbook or from topic to topic on a syllabus. Yet, the urgency to move on was strong in other content faculty I worked with, not just Carroll. The compulsion to get to the next topic or chapter was as constant as my desire to stay with the current one, to focus on language and comprehension, a reflection of the tension between coverage and learning.

Another obstacle to negotiating the curriculum and following the students' pace is that content faculty were sometimes reluctant to offer the assistance students needed, either because they thought students should already know how to do what they were being asked or because they did not know how to help. "I take these mental operations for granted," Carroll admitted during one of the faculty meetings, indicating that he was not used to attending to learning but was, rather, focused on teaching. When the curriculum or an assignment is negotiated and students are asked to carry out in-class writing tasks, the feedback is immediate; the teacher can observe problems as they arise and intervene on the spot. But content faculty in various linked classes were not always prepared to respond "at the point of need" (Nelson, 1991).

Before exploring the tension between teaching and learning in another FWP course, I now bring in an example of student resistance in the EAP writing class just discussed, in the form of an unanticipated refusal by some students to read the book I had chosen for that class. This illustrates another type of negotiation between teachers and students, one that occurred when my choice of a text was challenged and then supplanted by students' proposal for a more situated assignment.

DISSENT IN AN EAP WRITING CLASS

The examples of student resistance in this book have, so far, been from content classes. Yet, students also dissent in EAP classes, as illustrated by reactions to my choice of Mathabane's (1989) *Kaffir Boy in America* as the text for the writing class. As mentioned earlier, I chose that book to prepare students for the institutionally mandated writing assessment test given at the end of the semester, an argumentative essay on social issues. Mathabane, a South African tennis star who emigrated to the United States, offers vivid anecdotes about his experience as a black man, both in his home and adopted countries. His book includes chapters on attending college, dating, and bringing family members to the United States, issues students generally enjoy discussing and writing about. However, this particular book elicited a negative reaction in a few students, due, in part to a desire among some of the white students to distance themselves from the plight of black immigrants. They did not want to consider race as an issue, preferring to maintain an optimistic attitude toward U.S. life. Mikhail expresses this view most clearly in responding to my request for written feedback about the EAP class, a few weeks into the semester and a few chapters into *Kaffir Boy in America*:

If this is a writing class, why do we have to read the book that (in my opinion nobody in the class like). Why do we have to learn about some South African person who came to America and posses some kind of problems or enjoement. I don't want to learn about that. I'm sick and tired to read about his experience. I will never understand him or trying to get into his skin to understand it. I will never have that kind of problems that he does.

Mikhail's reference to nobody in the class liking the book was not borne out by feedback from two students, one Chinese and one Ghanaian, who wrote that they enjoyed the book. However, it is true that a few other students wrote that they did not want to continue reading *Kaffir Boy*. For example, here is Galya's feedback:

I don't understand why you choose this book. It is more good [there is better] American literature, British literature. Why in all classes (I mean also in reading class) you remind us that we are immigrants? We would like know more about American life, because we choose this country for our new life.

Mikhail is uninterested in "some South African person" and refuses to "get into his skin to understand" his experience. Like Chen's and Sasha's reactions to studying anorexia, discussed in chapter 5, Mikhail does not want to consider problems that he does not have. For her part, Galya does not consider Mathabane's memoir to be a worthy text, implying that "literature" is not produced by Africans.

Faced with these troubling reactions, I could have insisted that the class continue reading *Kaffir Boy in America* and that they explore their negative reactions, to uncover possible subtexts. This was the choice I made in pursuing a discussion of the 1998 murder of Matthew Shepard, an openly gay U.S. university student, despite the protest of one young man in the class and negative remarks by others (Benesch, 1999b). In that case, their dissent became a focus of discussion, a way to work through students' varied responses to the topic, leading initially dismissive reactions to become more nuanced. For example, the young man who was reluctant to even read an article about the murder, later explored his confusion about the relationship between heterosexuality and homosexuality, wondering if it was possible for a straight man to become gay. Other male students examined how their relationships with male friends had changed in light of U.S. homophobia due to a reluctance to be labeled homosexual. The lively and engaged dialogue in that class indicated that the choice to continue discussing the topic rather than give into the reluctance of some students paid off in greater understanding and empathy.

However, in the case of reactions to *Kaffir Boy in America* and to these particular linked classes, conditions seemed to favor abandoning the text. First, there was the sense that several students did not want to read about problems encountered by immigrants but, instead, about more hopeful aspects of life in the United States, those that had fortified them during the difficult process of leaving their homes. In addition, many students felt that they were not getting enough direct practice in the format of the upcoming proficiency test. Reading the text, they said, was a distraction from that practice rather than a useful trigger for writing about social issues as I had hoped it would be. Yet as important as either of these issues was that several students reported feeling uncomfortable in the linked classes, due to the tendency of students to group themselves according to language and cultural backgrounds. Russians sat with Russians, Chinese with Chinese and so on, leaving those who were the only members of their particular background feeling left out.

These issues emerged during the whole-class discussion of the written feedback, including the question of whether the students should continue reading *Kaffir Boy in America*. My dilemma was that I was reluctant to give into the sentiments expressed by Mikhail and Galya and to give up an opportunity to study the varying experiences of white immigrants and immigrants of color in the United States as well as these two students' assumptions about Mathabane, African writers, literature, and so on. However, I also recognized that the class needed to solve its own segregation problem. I therefore had to give up the idea that I could somehow make Mikhail, Galya, and others come to terms with racial discrimination, realizing that the text did not provide the context for that type of understanding. Rather than insisting on that agenda, I attended to concerns students had expressed about the class: too much focus on the immigrant experience; not enough focus on the writing test; and polarized social dynamics.

To address the latter problem, I urged the students to develop a solution. They came up with an assignment they called "Cultural Interviews," designed to break up the present seating arrangements and social dynamics. For this assignment, conducted over 3 weeks, pairs of students from two different cultural backgrounds first met to brainstorm topics about which they would interview each other. Next, they carried out the interviews, took notes, and wrote a paragraph about each topic. They then went to the library with their partners to do fact-checking. Then they wrote papers based on the information gathered and finally presented the results to the whole class in an oral presentation.

In accepting this assignment developed by the students, I also agreed to drop *Kaffir Boy in America*, believing that the cultural interviews assignment would make space for greater tolerance in a way that the text I had chosen had not. It also allowed them to select their own texts, ones they would need to carry out the assignment. Finally, I fulfilled the students' request to give direct practice in the writing assessment test format by assigning weekly argumentative essays.

The negotiation just described, prompted by my request for feedback about the EAP class, is an example of self-scrutiny in critical pedagogy. It shows how I reconsidered my choice of text in light of students' concerns. Yet, I am not suggesting that every time students complain about a text, I am willing to drop it. Indeed, I did not abandon the topic of anorexia in response to Chen's complaints about *The Best Little Girl in the World* or Sasha's lack of interest in the topic of anorexia. However, in the case of this particular EAP class, I decided that because of the tension among students, it made more sense for them to carry out their alternative assignment than to continue reading a book that seemed to impede dialogue. Most important of all, though, was the negotiation itself. Students were asked their opinions and when they came up with workable solutions to the problems at hand, the syllabus was revised to take their concerns into account.

I now turn to one more example from a different linked class to illustrate the difficulty of negotiating the relationship between teaching and learning across the curriculum.

RELATING TEACHING AND LEARNING

An example from another FWP block (ESL reading, ESL writing, and social science) illustrates the tension between teaching and learning even more dramatically than the first example. In this case, the social science teacher, Hardy, was a political scientist; the focus of the content course was "Power and Society." Hardy's interesting course description was intended to encourage students to think of themselves as active and critical shapers of civic life:

> This course is designed to investigate social science issues and problems by engaging you, the participant, with the following question: What kind of society would you like to live in, and how do you think particular social problems or issues should be resolved? We will explore various social issues and problems, such as human rights, democracy, equality, justice, education, gender roles, racism, income distribution, and power. As the student, you will need to find out what is generally known (and thought) about these issues, while at the same time assessing what you think can be done with the information you obtain to create the "good" society.

Professor Hardy and I attended many of each others' classes; mine was an EAP reading class. In his course, there were lively whole-class discussions of textbook chapters students had read for homework, with Hardy elaborating examples found in the text or offering others not appearing in the text. He gave two open-book exams, a midterm and a final, each consisting of two questions to be answered in essay form. After reading the midterms, Hardy told me that, generally speaking, students had not provided sufficient detail in their answers but, instead had written global statements in response to exam questions requiring greater specificity. He had wanted them to offer examples to illustrate abstract concepts, such as liberalism and democracy:

> I expected more elaboration, an indication they had thought about it. They didn't give me more than we talked about in class . . . the bare basics. I wanted them to include material from the book we hadn't talked about. Everything [in their answers] came from the lecture. I want to know they can get information from the book. Lectures make it possible for them to read and get more detail from the chapters, more examples. (Hardy, personal communication, November 1998)

When I pointed out to Hardy that he had not explained to students about the importance of offering examples not discussed in the lectures, he said, "I assumed they knew that."

Observing that students needed greater instruction in how to provide more detail and examples in their written answers, I worked more closely on the relationship between generalization and exemplification in the reading class, underscoring the point that this would be required not only on the writing assessment test but also on the social science final. I also thought that students should be shown explicitly how to find examples in their textbook and elaborate them in the context of an essay exam, especially material not discussed in class. Therefore, I asked Hardy if we could run a review class together in which we would work with students in groups on locating examples in the textbook and in their own experience to support arguments they would be making, in preparation for the upcoming final exam.

He agreed to participate in the review session and assigned students to groups according to grades they had received on the midterm: those who had received A and B grades met with each other; those with lower scores met with us. Yet, during the session, he exhibited discomfort with the process of breaking down the test questions and having students locate areas in the text that might help answer them. That is, although he was accustomed to giving his students exam questions beforehand so they could prepare to answer them on the day of the exam, he was reluctant to guide them through the process during the preparation class to help them formulate more detailed responses. Despite his reluctance to offer this instruction in the study groups, we followed through with our plan to show students how to write responses to questions on the upcoming exam with examples and sufficient detail. We asked them to search for places in the textbook where the answers might appear and to discern the details in those places so that they might include them on their exams. They rehearsed their answers out loud, using talk as prewriting.

Perhaps due to this close work done in the review groups, students' scores on the final exam were higher than they had been on the midterm. However, Hardy told me that he had not wanted to lead students so explicitly to what he wanted them to achieve on their own. He wished they had been able to do it without his help.

This experience left me asking: If students do not already know how to perform tasks on which they are being evaluated, when and how are they supposed to learn to do that work? If the focus in academic content classes is on teaching a body of knowledge rather than on how to make sense of it, how are students going to learn that content? How do EAP teachers enhance the relationship between teaching and learning?

PREPARATION FOR WHAT?

When teachers lecture, they have no access to students' thinking, to their comprehension or lack of comprehension. There are no immediate feedback mechanisms informing the teacher about whether or not individual students understand. Teachers may ask if students have questions, but those who are most confused may not know what to ask to clear up their confusion (Lynch, 1993). They may be so lost that a teacher's answer to a single question would not offer the required guidance.

When, on the other hand, teachers invite students to discuss and write about course material, they may discover that students have not understood what they have read in the textbook or heard in a lecture (Mayher, Lester, & Pradl, 1983). Yet, will the teacher then be prepared to help students make sense of the material or, instead, assume that students should do it on their own or that they should have already learned from their prior educational experience how to read and understand the material they are now presented with? Will they assume that reading and writing are skills that are easily transferable from one context to another, or instead get involved in the learning processes particular to the content students are meeting in their class?

My research on linked classes (Benesch, 1996, 1999a) has led me to the following conclusion: If there are no institutional mechanisms in place for guiding students through the difficulties of understanding and interrogating new material, EAP teachers should encourage students to organize for teaching that is more carefully connected to their learning. Two examples of organizing students have been presented in this book. In chapter 6, I described the delegation, a group I urged students to join in order to formulate and articulate their concerns about the number of upcoming anthropology assignments due in the short amount of time remaining in the semester. The delegation was the culmination of community-building in that linked course where students learned to work together to meet the limit-situations presented by the anthropology class. In chapter 7, I discussed an EAP assignment asking students to write proposals for changes in the psychology class, based on their informal complaints. In these two cases, I acted as an advocate for students because I believed that without the type of encouragement provided, students would internalize a sense of private failure and inadequacy. My goal in the EAP class was to ensure that students would work collectively to get the type of instruction they needed. In addition, there is an example in this chapter showing EAP students organizing themselves to find an alternative assignment to a book they did not find useful in preparing them for the upcoming writing proficiency test.

Raimes (1985) has demonstrated that non-native undergraduates in U.S. colleges need "more time; more opportunity to talk, listen, read, and write in order to marshal the vocabulary they need to make their own background knowledge available to them in their L2" (p. 250). Sternglass's (1997) longitudinal research of basic writers at CUNY led to a similar conclusion, pointing to the importance of talking and writing in all courses across the curriculum, not just language and composition courses. Yet, these findings about allowing for more time, talking, and writing have been incorporated into the instruction of non-native students only sporadically at CUNY, the university where Raimes and I both teach and where Sternglass taught previously. Although linking language and content courses as a way to mainstream ESL students occurs in most CUNY colleges, the trend since the mid-1990s has been to construct ESL as remediation and identify ESL students as those who must prepare themselves for college *before* being admitted into academic programs.

Contrary to research pointing to the need for more time and better-contextualized language instruction, CUNY's ESL students are increasingly being offered precollege, noncredit teaching divorced from academic course work and expected to apply what they learn in those settings to a completely different context, content courses across the curriculum. The regression from more-contextualized to less-contextualized ESL instruction and the sorting of students into ready and not-ready categories is due to the political climate of downsizing public higher education by keeping out immigrants and minority students. Opposing the regressive politics of exclusion in New York State's institutions of public higher education, Assemblyman Ed Sullivan, an advocate of open admissions, declared on public radio: "The premise of democracy is that everyone is ready. Anyone who says some people aren't ready is attacking democracy." A former ESL teacher himself, Sullivan supports offering L2 instruction in full-time college programs rather than in remedial, noncredit settings.

CUNY Professor Ricardo Otheguy believes that invoking standards is a way to exclude language minority students from education. He opposes the "frontloading" of assessment (Otheguy, 1999), that is, the use of proficiency tests to sort university applicants, finding that this process serves to depress the aspirations of immigrants, encouraging them to take low-pay, low-skill jobs. Part of organizing students for more-contextualized instruction is helping them analyze the political situations in which they find themselves so they can understand academic life in the larger political and economic context (Benesch, 1996).

SUMMARY

The examples in this chapter demonstrate obstacles to dialogic teaching. One is the tradition of covering material regardless of whether students have understood previously introduced concepts. This includes the habit of following a schedule dictated by a syllabus, a textbook, and tests rather than students' pace, understanding, and questions. It is based on an assumption that students, even those in introductory general education courses, should grasp new material readily, allowing the teacher to move on quickly, not to dwell on a single topic for any length of time.

One way to break through the coverage tradition is to give students opportunities to organize themselves to bring about teaching more attuned to their pace. Critical EAP teachers can encourage students to challenge the construction of EAP students as underprepared, remedial, or deficient, and to demand more appropriate texts and pedagogy. It can engage students in needs and rights analysis by asking for feedback, including proposals for change. It can act on those proposals by working out solutions with the students.

I asked for written feedback from the students in the first linked course discussed in this chapter by posing the following questions: What do you like most about this class? What do you like least about the class? What suggestions do you have to improve the class? They offered various responses but what stood out was the conflict produced by the text I had chosen, *Kaffir Boy in America*. In the follow-up discussion, some students argued that the text was not appropriate for this particular class and they proposed an alternative reading/writing assignment situated in their observations about the segregated dynamics in the linked courses. After weighing my concerns about abandoning the text and their concerns about preparing for the writing exam and the classroom climate, I accepted their proposals.

This example shows that despite the challenges of dialogic teaching, there are also possibilities for students' active participation. Institutional constraints are undeniable, yet they do not block resistance or openings for transformation. Critical EAP teachers' roles in encouraging change have been outlined in each of the chapters. The next and final chapter discusses implications for instruction of the three imagined audiences of this book: EAP teachers, content teachers, and critical teachers.

Chapter 9

What is and What Might Be: Instructional Implications for EAP, Content, and Critical Teachers

TOWARD AN ETHICS OF EAP

EAP is at the point in its history where it is ready to consider its ethics. Up to now, the focus has been on getting jobs done, no matter whose goals are being fulfilled or what the consequences might be. Developing an ethics of EAP requires a reckoning with how the field positions itself vis-à-vis institutions, programs, funding agencies, academic classes, and students. It calls for greater discussion of what jobs EAP teachers are willing to accept, basing their decisions not solely on financial considerations or the attractive perquisites of international travel. It calls for further consideration of the role of EAP teachers: Are they to be trainers, carrying out target aims uncritically, or educators, in the Freirean sense, imagining with students a more just world? Or both? How might EAP relate needs and rights in their analysis of the target? Will EAP teachers act as advocates for inclusion or will they enact exclusionary policies aimed at keeping out nonelite students? Will they construct EAP exclusively as academic and workplace preparation or also as a place where students can shape and transform what is being offered to them?

Traditional EAP's ideology of pragmatism does not raise concerns about the relationship of EAP teachers to official curricula, pedagogy, and assessment. Instead, it assumes that their role is to prepare students for the requirements they face or will face in their academic classes. This political position appears as neutral because it upholds the status quo, yet it is no more neutral than one that interrogates existing demands and assumptions (Benesch, 1993).

Myles Horton (1990), founder of the Highlander Folk School in Tennessee, USA, explains the myth of neutrality as the normalizing of the status quo and shows that political choices are unavoidable in the course of living:

> Neutrality is just another word for accepting the status quo as universal law. You either choose to go along with the way things are, or you reject the status quo. Then you're forced to think through what you believe. If you're going to be for something, then you have to know there's an opposite that you're against. That runs contrary to the traditional thinking in this country [the US]: you're supposed to be positive, for something but not against something. But it's impossible to be for anything without being against something. You have to clarify what you're against, and once that's figured out, you have to determine how to do something about it. You say, "OK, this is the kind of world I'd like to see, these are the kinds of values that seem important to me." Then you have to figure out how to work so that it affects people. (Horton 1990, pp. 139–140)

Horton, a social activist, offers a blueprint for how to think ethically. He begins with an assumption: You either accept the way things are as natural and inevitable, or you call the status quo in to question. Once you decide to interrogate the way things are, you consider alternatives, based on the type of world you believe is just, thereby clarifying your values. Next, you seek actions to enact those values.

Horton (1990) describes the relationship between what is and what might be as the operation of two eyes. Teachers train one eye on students to discern what they are concerned with, in the "here and now." They focus the other eye on a more promising future, a world where equality and democracy prevail.

I hope this book will encourage EAP teachers to continue focusing on the specific requirements of target situations, to offer courses taking needs in to account. Yet, I also hope they will reserve a second eye for changes that might bring about better conditions in academic life, in workplaces, and in the societies in which they teach and live.

In this chapter, I offer some implications for teaching for three different audiences: EAP teachers, content teachers, and critical teachers. These suggestions aim to balance what is and what might be.

IMPLICATIONS FOR EAP TEACHERS

One of my goals here is to problematize reductive views of critical pedagogy expressed in EAP publications and presentations. At conferences, I have heard everything from "Critical teaching is getting students to march in the streets" to "Critical teaching is the imposition of the teacher's political agenda," to "Critical teaching is letting students choose their own topics," indicating that for some it is political indoctrination while for others it is simply student-centered teaching. The examples in Part II show that critical teaching takes on a variety of forms depending on the local context and political climate. That is, it is situated in the particular needs and rights of students in the setting in which it is carried out. For example, critical teaching may lead students to request more equitable conditions, as was the case of the delegation discussed in chapter 6, or to demonstrate with their teachers against tuition increases, as some of my students did in 1995. Yet, it is not exclusively oppositional but, rather, responsive to the demands of the target situation while being open to the possibility of questioning them.

Misconceptions about critical EAP have arisen, in part, by ignoring the centrality in this pedagogy of Freire's theory of hope. Freire did not intend for teachers to mine their societies for problems and then present them to students who would then be paralyzed by despair. Hope is central to Freire's politics and pedagogy: "I do not understand human existence, and the struggle needed to improve it, apart from hope and dream. Hope is an ontological need" (Freire, 1994, p. 9). Overlooking hope as a theoretical construct has led some to view critical pedagogy as a negative and depressing enterprise, aiming to convince students to take up social issues that preoccupy their teachers. Thus, at the 1994 TESOL conference, for instance, using the conceit of "something old, something new, something borrowed, something blue" to discuss different types of ESL composition instruction, one presenter characterized critical pedagogy as something blue, that is, as assigning depressing topics—homelessness, pollution, nuclear proliferation—rather than topics the students might have chosen on their own. However, as noted, that view of critical teaching does not acknowledge its grounding in the idea of hope, and another important concept, situatedness. It assumes that the curriculum emerges from the teacher's outside political interests, regardless of the situation in which the teacher and students find themselves. From that point of view, my assigning anorexia to EAP students could be seen as indoctrination rather than as a situated response to the masculinist curriculum of the linked psychology lecture course, an attempt to balance its syllabus to include an issue of possible concern to female students (see chap. 5).

My goal in trying to clear up some misperceptions about critical pedagogy is not to convince EAP teachers to "go" critical. Critical pedagogy is a response to disaffection with the status quo, not a current trend or new method of teaching looking for converts. It will appeal to teachers who are unhappy with current conditions, seeking ways to bring about pedagogical, institutional, and social change on behalf of and with their students. It offers practical ways to help students organize for change.

My interest in critical pedagogy grew from the particular limit-situations I faced as an EAP teacher in a publicly funded institution whose budget was diminishing, leading to larger classes, fewer full-time teaching lines, and greater restrictions on open enrollment. In addition, the pedagogy I observed in content classes was mainly lecturing, attributable in part to growing class size but also to tradition. Therefore, during the first few years I taught linked classes, I hoped to encourage content faculty to assign more writing, allow for more student talk, and follow the students' pace of learning. However, as illustrated in chapters 7 and 8, these attempts proved somewhat discouraging, and I therefore turned to helping students organize for the types of changes they seemed to be calling for in their complaints and resistant behaviors. I encouraged them to seek relief from the alienation they were expressing, by claiming membership in the institution to which they had been accepted. I believed that if they organized with other students for change in an academic setting, they might do the same in various aspects of their lives and in other settings.

Although I do not think the results of my experiments are transferable to other settings, I believe that critical EAP practice includes helping students organize themselves for what Boomer (1992) calls the *demystification of learning*, which includes making explicit the power relations, values, and assumptions on which teaching in particular institutions is based. Included in this demystification is encouraging students to speak up when they do not understand and to make it clear that they expect their questions to be taken seriously, not ignored in the name of coverage or impatience with their pace of learning. In this formulation, students are not novices, or outsiders, who must surrender to the language and practices of academic discourse communities; rather, they are active members of the academy whose rights should be considered. This does not mean that students are required to speak up but that this option should be available.

The principles just outlined might be incorporated into EAP practices in both linked and unlinked classes. They make room for rights analysis to address limit-situations along with the more traditional needs analysis usually carried out.

IMPLICATIONS FOR CONTENT TEACHERS

The examples in the book show teaching in five different undergraduate content classes (two psychology lecture classes, one anthropology course, and two introduction to social science classes). In three of those classes, writing was assigned by the content teachers as a way to engage students with the material. In two, lectures were the dominant mode of presenting material, although students were encouraged to ask questions. However, the requirement to cover numerous topics was a common feature of four of the content classes, creating difficulties for the content teachers and students alike. Teachers were restricted in the amount of students talk they could allow, and students were frustrated by the limitations on questions, whole-class discussion, and small-group work.

I am not optimistic about changes in the traditional regime of teacher coverage of large amounts of material. Academic institutions, especially publicly funded ones, operate under severe financial and political constraints, making curriculum negotiation and reform difficult. Growing class size, standardized tests, pressure from licensing boards to introduce a certain number of topics, and the speeded-up climate of the information age limit dialogue and depth of presentation of academic material. These limitations are real and cannot be ignored, but they do not exclude possibilities for change. I hope the examples in this book encourage content teachers to link their courses to EAP courses, creating more time and space for students to make sense of new concepts and interrogate the material they are offered. That is, it may not be necessary to attempt large-scale change in educational institutions for content teaching to become more responsive to non-native speaking students and for EAP teachers to contextualize their instruction by linking it to content courses.

The examples in Part II illustrate the tension between dialogue and coverage, an issue that can be taken up when EAP and content teachers link their classes. They might ask: How many topics have to be covered in one semester? What should be the ratio of teacher to student talk? Should time be set aside for students to talk to each other about the material? Can students' questions be the basis for any of the lectures? How might writing be used as a tool for learning? Are there multiple assessment measures taking various learning styles into account? Discussion of these questions acknowledges the challenges of learning content in a new language and the possibility of interaction between language and content teachers in promoting greater inclusion and depth of learning.

The relationship between teaching content and teaching language might also be an area of discussion between EAP and content teachers. They could talk about how academic power relations tend to position EAP as a service to content demands and about possible alternatives to that positioning. In doing so, they might reveal their assumptions about respective responsibilities, perhaps educating each other about the challenges of doing their jobs. Rather than automatically assuming a one-way transfer of information from content teacher to students with EAP bolstering that type of teaching, they might consider ways both classes could facilitate student participation and inquiry, through talking and writing.

IMPLICATIONS FOR CRITICAL TEACHERS

Some ESL teachers with an interest in critical pedagogy might be put off by the sometimes lofty theory, especially when it is not illuminated by examples of how the theory could be enacted. For example, Johnston (1999) explores his discomfort with what he considers critical pedagogists' revolutionary claims, finding these to exaggerate the type of change that might actually be brought about in academic institutions. The problem

Johnston identifies can be addressed by offering illustrations of critical practice showing the relationship between critical theory and complicated and messy classrooms in highly regulated academic institutions. Then, it becomes possible for theorists to incorporate these complications to reflect both its utopian vision and the pragmatic realities of classrooms, including the limit-situations of institutional life.

Although there is interest in having more examples of critical pedagogy, Aronowitz (1993, 1998), Aronowitz and Giroux (1991), and Brady (1994) have raised concerns about the risks of domesticating critical theory by turning it into a depoliticized method of instruction. For example, Aronowitz (1993) warns about the "fetish of method" (p. 8), that is, the tendency of North American educators to claim that their student-centered classes are enactments of critical theory, when in fact the teachers have simply increased the amount of student talk and writing, stripping away the theory's political basis. Aronowitz and Giroux (1991) warn against a version of critical pedagogy focused exclusively on "dialogue, process, and exchange" with no sense of a larger political project that challenges the status quo of social and economic inequality (p. 117). Brady (1994) objects to applying Freire's theories in a context other than the one in which they were developed, finding this to be an act of appropriation and domestication "as part of a Western hegemonic project" (p. 151).

Clearly these concerns must be addressed. Critical and progressive pedagogies should not be conflated nor should student-centered teaching be misconstrued as critical. Critical pedagogy is a political project, not a method aiming to "motivate students to imbibe the curriculum with enthusiasm" (Aronowitz, 1993, p. 11). However, I worry that those who want to teach critically could be discouraged by these caveats, fearful of "contaminating" theory by misapplying it to their own practice, thus creating a further split between critical theory and practice. Without examples of critical practice for scrutiny and reflection, critical theory becomes an abstract description of an unattainable utopian project. In my opinion, it is riskier to ossify critical theory in an attempt to preserve its political purity, than it is for some student-centered teachers to mistakenly claim to be critical teachers.

Judging from my own experience, critical teachers often ask themselves if what they are attempting in the classroom is truly critical. That is, they are not satisfied with merely introducing student-centered techniques, but want to be sure that they actively keep alive the question of whether they are living up to critical theory's intellectual, political, and pedagogical promises. When trying to teach EAP critically, I wonder whether I really am a critical teacher or merely a progressive one, satisfied with incremental and observable changes in the present context. Is it enough, I ask myself, for students to organize themselves to change classroom conditions? How do the more pragmatic activities figure into a larger political project? How do I balance students' needs and rights?

These questions are not instances of private self-doubt, leading to abandoning the experiment, but instead are a necessary part of critical praxis, what Pennycook (1999) calls its "self-reflexive stance" (p. 345), that is, questioning the theory, practice, content, and politics of one's own experiments. Problematizing practice is a feature of critical pedagogy, allowing the theory to guide teaching, and teaching to complicate theory.

Fortunately, there is a growing body of critical ESL literature offering well-theorized examples in a variety of settings (Auerbach, Barahona, Midy, Vaquerano, Zambrano, & Arnaud, 1996; Auerbach & McGrail, 1991; Ibrahim, 1999; Morgan, 1998; Moriarty, 1998; Nelson, 1999; Vandrick, 1995). An entire issue of the *TESOL Quarterly*, edited by Pennycook (1999), is devoted to critical approaches to TESOL, signaling increased interest in this area of research and teaching. This book is offered as a contribution to that literature in the hope that it will encourage EAP students and teachers to work for a more equitable world, guided by a sense of community and justice.

REFERENCES

Allen, P., & Widdowson, H. (1974). *English in the physical sciences.* London: Oxford University Press.

Allison, D. (1994). Comments on Sarah Benesch's "ESL, ideology, and the politics of pragmatism": A reader reacts. *TESOL Quarterly, 28,* 618–623.

Allison, D. (1996). Pragmatist discourse and English for academic purposes. *English for Specific Purposes, 15,* 85–103.

Anderson, G. L., & Irvine, P. (1993). Informing critical literacy with ethnography. In C. Lankshear & P. L. McLaren (Eds.), *Critical literacy: Politics, praxis, and the postmodern* (pp. 81–104). Albany: State University of New York Press.

Angeloni, E. (Ed.). (1997). *Annual Editions: Anthropology 97/98.* Guilford, CT: Dushkin Publishing Group/Brown & Benchmark.

Araujo Freire, A. M. (1994). Notes. In P. Freire, *Pedagogy of hope: Reliving pedagogy of the oppressed* (pp. 205–240). New York: Continuum.

Aronowitz, S. (1993). Paulo Freire's radical democratic humanism. In P. McLaren & P. Leonard (Eds.), *Paulo Freire: A critical encounter* (pp. 8–24). London: Routledge.

Aronowitz, S. (1998). Introduction. In P. Freire, *Pedagogy of Freedom: Ethics, democracy, and civic courage* (pp. 1–19). Lanham, MD: Rowman & Littlefield.

Aronowitz, S., & Giroux, H. A. (1991). *Postmodern education: Politics, culture, and social criticism.* Minneapolis: University of Minnesota Press.

Atkinson, D. (1997). A critical approach to critical thinking in TESOL. *TESOL Quarterly, 31,* 71–94.

Atkinson, D. (1998). Comments on Dwight Atkinson's "A Critical Approach to Critical Thinking in TESOL": The author responds. *TESOL Quarterly, 29,* 133–137.

Atkinson, D. (1999). Comments on Ryuko Kubota's "Japanese culture constructed by discourses: Implications for applied linguistics research and ELT." Another reader reacts. *TESOL Quarterly, 33,* 745–749.

Atkinson, D., & Ramanathan, V. (1995). Cultures of writing: An ethnographic comparison of L1 and L2 university writing/language programs. *TESOL Quarterly, 29,* 539–568.

Auerbach, E., & McGrail, L. (1991). Rosa's challenge: Connecting classroom and community contexts. In S. Benesch (Ed.), *ESL in America: Myths and possibilities* (pp. 96–111). Portsmouth, NH: Boynton/Cook Heinemann.

Auerbach, E., Barahona, B., Midy, J., Vaquerano, F., Zambrano, A., & Arnaud, J. (1996). *Adult ESL literacy from the community to the community: A guide book for participatory literacy training.* Mahwah, NJ: Lawrence Erlbaum Associates.

Axline, V. M. (1964). *Dibs in search of self.* New York: Ballantine Books.

Barber, C. L. (1962). Some measurable characteristics of modern scientific prose. Reprinted in J. Swales (Ed.), *Episodes in ESP: A source and reference book on the development of English for science and technology* (pp. 3–14). Hemel Hempstead, UK: Prentice-Hall International.

Barron, C. (1992). Cultural syntonicity: Co-operative relationships between the ESP unit and other departments. *Hong Kong Papers in Linguistics and Language Teaching, 15,* 1–14. (ERIC Document Reproduction Service No. 355 766).

Bartky, S. L. (1988). Foucault, femininity, and the modernization of patriarchal power. In I. Diamond & L. Quinby (Eds.), *Feminisms and Foucault: Reflections and resistance* (pp. 61–86). Boston: Northeastern University Press.

Bazerman, C. (1988). *Shaping written knowledge: The genre and activity of the experimental article in science.* Madison: University of Wisconsin Press.

Benesch, S. (1988). Linking content and language teachers: Collaboration across the curriculum. In S. Benesch (Ed.), *Ending remediation: Linking ESL and content in higher education* (pp. 57–66). Washington, DC: TESOL.

Benesch, S. (1991). ESL on campus: Questioning testing and tracking policies. In S. Benesch (Ed.), *ESL in America: Myths and possibilities* (pp. 59–74). Portsmouth, NH: Boynton/Cook Heinemann.

Benesch, S. (1992). Sharing responsibilities: An alternative to the adjunct model. *College ESL, 2,* 1–10.

Benesch, S. (1993). ESL, ideology, and the politics of pragmatism. *TESOL Quarterly, 27,* 705–717.

Benesch, S. (1996). Needs analysis and curriculum development in EAP: An example of a critical approach. *TESOL Quarterly, 30,* 723–738.

Benesch, S. (1998). Anorexia: A feminist EAP curriculum. In T. Smoke (Ed.), *Adult ESL: Politics, pedagogy, and participation in classrooms and community programs* (pp. 101–114). Mahwah, NJ: Lawrence Erlbaum Associates.

Benesch, S. (1999a). Rights analysis: Studying power relations in an academic setting. *English for Specific Purposes, 18,* 313–327.

Benesch, S. (1999b). Thinking critically, thinking dialogically. *TESOL Quarterly, 33,* 573–580.

Benson, M. J. (1989). The academic listening task: A case study. *TESOL Quarterly, 23,* 421–445.

Benson, M. J. (1991). University ESL reading: A content analysis. *English for Specific Purposes, 10,* 75–88.

Berkenkotter, C., & Huckin, T. N. (1995). *Genre knowledge in disciplinary communication.* Mahwah, NJ: Lawrence Erlbaum Associates.

Berlin, J. A. (1988). Rhetoric and ideology in the writing class. *College English, 50,* 477–494.

Bhatia, V. K. (1993). *Analyzing genre: Language use in professional settings.* Essex: Longman.

Blakely, R. (1995). The English language fellows program. *College ESL, 5,* 1–20.

Boomer, G. (1992). Negotiating the curriculum. In G. Boomer, N. Lester, C. Onore, & J. Cook (Eds.), *Negotiating the curriculum: Educating for the 21st century* (pp. 4–14). London: Falmer Press.

Bordo, S. (1993). *Unbearable weight: Feminism, western culture, and the body.* Berkeley: University of California Press.

Bosher, S., & Rowenkamp, L. (1998). The refugee/immigrant in higher education: The role of educational background. *College ESL, 8,* 23–42.

Brady, J. (1994). Critical literacy, feminism, and a politics of representation. In P. L. McLaren & C. Lankshear (Eds.), *Politics of liberation: Paths from Freire* (pp. 142–153). London: Routledge.

Braine, G. (1988). A reader reacts (commentary on Ruth Spack's "Initiating ESL students into the academic discourse community: How far should we go?"). *TESOL Quarterly, 22,* 700–702.

Britton, J. (1982). How we got here. In G. Pradl (Ed.), *Prospect and retrospect: Selected essays of James Britton* (pp. 169–184). Montclair, NJ: Boynton/Cook Publishers.

Britton, J., Burgess, T., Martin, N., McLeod, A., & Rosen, H. (1975). *The development of writing abilities* (pp. 11–18). London: Macmillan Education for the Schools Council.

Candlin, C. (1999, March). *English for specific purposes—program development for the new millennium.* Paper presented at 33rd annual TESOL Convention, New York.

Cherryholmes, C. H. (1988). *Power and criticism: Poststructural investigations in education.* New York: Teachers College Press.

Cherryholmes, C. H. (1999). *Reading pragmatism.* New York: Teachers College Press.

Cummins, J., & Sayers, D. (1995). *Brave new schools: Challenging cultural illiteracy through global networks.* New York: St. Martin's.

CUNY ESL Task Force Report. (1994). CUNY, Office of Academic Affairs. New York: The City University of New York.

Diamond, I., & Quinby, L. (1988). American feminism and the language of control. In I. Diamond & L. Quinby (Eds.), *Feminisms and Foucault: Reflections and resistance* (pp. 193–206). Boston: Northeastern University Press.

Doctorow, E. L. (1974). *Ragtime.* New York: Plume.

Drobnic, K. (1978). *Teaching conceptual paragraphs in EST courses: A practical technique.* (ERIC Document Reproduction Service No. ED 249 766).

Dudley-Evans, T. (1995). Common-core and specific approaches to the teaching of academic writing. In D. Belcher & G. Braine (Eds.), *Academic writing in a second language: Essays on research and pedagogy* (pp. 293–312). Norwood, NJ: Ablex.

Dudley-Evans, T., & St. John, M. J. (1998). *Developments in English for specific purposes: A multidisciplinary approach.* Cambridge, England: Cambridge University Press.

Elbow, P. (1973). *Writing without teachers.* New York: Oxford University Press.

Elbow, P. (1981). *Writing with power: Techniques for mastering the writing process.* New York: Oxford University Press.

Ewer, J., & Latorre, G. (1969). *A course in basic scientific English.* London: Longman.

Feldman, R. S. (1993). *Understanding psychology* (3rd ed.). New York: McGraw-Hill.

Flowerdew, J. (1990). English for specific purposes—A selective review of the literature. *ELT Journal, 44*(4), 326–337.

Foucault, M. (1977). *Discipline & punish: The birth of the prison.* New York: Vintage Books.

Foucault, M. (1980). Power & Strategies. In C. Gordon (Ed.), *Power/knowledge: Selected interviews and other writings, 1972–1977* (pp. 134–145). New York: Pantheon Books.

Foucault, M. (1980). The Eye of Power. In C. Gordon (Ed.), *Power/Knowledge: Selected interviews and other writings, 1972–1977* (pp. 146–165). New York: Pantheon Books.

Foucault, M. (1988). On Power. In L. D. Kritzman (Ed.), *Politics, philosophy, culture: Interviews and other writings, 1977–1984.* New York: Routledge.

Fox, H. (1994). *Listening to the world: Cultural issues in academic writing.* Urbana, IL: National Council of Teachers of English.

Freire, P. (1970). *Pedagogy of the oppressed.* New York: Continuum.

Freire, P. (1973). *Education for critical consciousness.* New York: Continuum.

Freire, P. (1994). *Pedagogy of hope: Reliving pedagogy of the oppressed.* New York: Continuum.

Freire, P. (1996). *Letters to Christina: Reflections on my life and work.* New York: Routledge.

Freire, P. (1998a). *Pedagogy of the heart.* New York: Continuum.

Freire, P. (1998b). *Pedagogy of freedom: Ethics, democracy, and civic courage.* Lanham, MD: Rowman & Littlefield.

Fulwiler, T., & Young, A. (Eds.). (1990). *Programs that work: Models and methods for writing across the curriculum.* Portsmouth, NH: Heinemann.

Geisler, C. (1994). *Academic literacy and the nature of expertise: Reading, writing, and knowing in academic philosophy.* Hillsdale, NJ: Lawrence Erlbaum Associates.

Giroux, H. A. (1997). *Pedagogy and the politics of hope: Theory, culture, and schooling.* Boulder, CO: Westview Press.

Gore, J. (1992). What we can do for you! What *can* "we" do for "you"? Struggling over empowerment in critical and feminist pedagogy. In C. Luke & J. Gore (Eds.), *Feminisms and critical pedagogy* (pp. 54–73). New York: Routledge.

Haas, T., Smoke, T., & Hernandez, J. (1991). A collaborative model for empowering nontraditional students. In S. Benesch (Ed.), *ESL in America: Myths and possibilities* (pp. 112–129). Portsmouth, NH: Boynton/Cook Heinemann.

Harklau, L., Losey, K. M., & Siegal, M. (1999). Linguistically diverse students and college writing: What is equitable and appropriate? In L. Harklau, K. M. Losey, & M. Siegal (Eds.), *Generation 1.5 meets college composition: Issues in the teaching of writing to U.S.-educated learners of ESL* (pp. 1–14). Mahwah, NJ: Lawrence Erlbaum Associates.

Heilbroner, R. L. (1992). *The making of economic society.* (9th ed.). New York: Prentice-Hall.

Herbert, A. J. (1965). *The structure of technical English.* London: Longman.

Hirsch, L. (1988). Language across the curriculum: A model for ESL students in content courses. In S. Benesch (Ed.), *Ending remediation: Linking ESL and content in higher education* (pp. 71–89). Washington, DC: TESOL.

History of E province: The oil giant of Saudi Aramco. (1992, March 30). *Moneyclips.*

Horowitz, D. (1986a). Process not product: Less than meets the eye. *TESOL Quarterly, 20,* 141–144.

Horowitz, D. (1986b). What professors actually require: Academic tasks for the ESL classroom. *TESOL Quarterly, 20,* 445–462.

Horton, M. (1990). *The long haul: An autobiography.* New York: Doubleday.

Huddlestone, R. D. (1971). *The sentence in written English.* Cambridge, England: Cambridge University Press.

Hutchinson, T., & Waters, A. (1987). *English for specific purposes: A learning-centered approach.* Cambridge: Cambridge University Press.

Hyon, S. (1996). Genre in three traditions: Implications for ESL. *TESOL Quarterly, 30,* 693–722.

Ibrahim, A. (1999). Becoming black: Rap and hip-hop, race, gender, identity, and the politics of ESL learning. *TESOL Quarterly, 33,* 349–369.

Jacoby, S., Leech, D. & Holten, C. (1995). A genre-based developmental writing course for undergraduate ESL science majors. In D. Belcher & G. Braine (Eds.), *Academic writing in a second language: Essays on research and pedagogy* (pp. 351–373). Norwood, NJ: Ablex.

JanMohammed, A. R. (1993). Some implications of Paulo Freire's border pedagogy. *Cultural Studies, 7*(1), 107–117.

Johns, A. M. (1981). Necessary English: A faculty survey. *TESOL Quarterly, 15,* 51–57.

Johns, A. M. (1988a). The discourse communities dilemma: Identifying transferable skills for the academic milieu. *English for Specific Purposes, 7,* 55–59.

Johns, A. M. (1988b). A reader reacts (commentary on Ruth Spack's "Initiating ESL students into the academic discourse community: How far should we go?"). *TESOL Quarterly, 22,* 705–707.

Johns, A. M. (1990a). Coherence as a cultural phenomenon: Employing ethnographic principles in the academic milieu. In U. Connor & A. M. Johns (Eds.), *Coherence in writing: Research and pedagogical perspectives* (pp. 209–226). Alexandria, VA: TESOL.

Johns, A. M. (1990b). L1 composition theories: Implications for developing theories of L2 composition. In B. Kroll (Ed.), *Second language writing: Research insights for the classroom* (pp. 24–36). Cambridge, England: Cambridge University Press.

Johns, A. M. (1995). Teaching classroom and authentic genres: Initiating students into academic cultures and discourses. In D. Belcher & G. Braine (Eds.), *Academic writing in a second language: Essays on research and pedagogy* (pp. 277–291). Norwood NJ: Ablex.

Johns, A. M. (1997). *Text, role, and context: Developing academic literacies.* Cambridge, England: Cambridge University Press.

Johns, A. M., & Dudley-Evans, T. (1991). English for specific purposes: International in scope, specific in purpose. *TESOL Quarterly, 25,* 297–314.

Johns, T. F. & Dudley-Evans, A. (1980). An experiment in team-teaching of overseas postgraduate students of transportation and plant biology. *Team Teaching in ESP. ELT Documents, 106,* 6–23.

Johnson, C. D. (1971). Presentation to the Beirut conference on adult English for national development. *Proceedings of conference on adult English for national development* (pp. 63–73). Beirut: Center for English Language Research and Teaching, the American University of Beirut. (ERIC Document Reproduction Service No. ED 130 525).

Johnston, B. (1999). Putting critical pedagogy in its place: A personal account. *TESOL Quarterly, 33,* 557–565.

Jordan, R. R. (1989). English for Academic Purposes (EAP). *Language Teaching, 22/3,* 150–164.

Jordan, R. R. (1997). *English for academic purposes: A guide and resource book for teachers.* Cambridge, England: Cambridge University Press.

Lackstrom, J., Selinker, L., & Trimble, L. (1973). Technical rhetorical principles and grammatical choice. *TESOL Quarterly, 7,* 127–136.

Lave, J. (1997). The culture of acquisition and the practice of understanding. In D. Kirshner & J. A. Whitson (Eds.), *Situated cognition: Social, semiotic, and psychological perspectives* (pp. 17–35). Mahwah, NJ: Lawrence Erlbaum Associates.

Leki, I. (1992). *Understanding ESL writers: A guide for teachers.* Portsmouth, NH: Boynton/Cook Heinemann.

Leki, I. (1995). Coping strategies of ESL students in writing tasks across the curriculum. *TESOL Quarterly, 29,* 235–258.

Leki, I. (1999). "Pretty much I screwed up": Ill-served needs of a permanent resident. In L. Harklau, K. M. Losey, & M. Siegal (Eds.), *Generation 1.5 meets college composition: Issues in the teaching of writing to U.S.- educated learners of ESL* (pp. 17–43). Mahwah, NJ: Lawrence Erlbaum Associates.

Leki, I., & Carson, J. (1997). "Completely different worlds": EAP and the writing experiences of ESL students in university courses. *TESOL Quarterly, 31,* 39–69.

Levenkron, S. (1978). *The best little girl in the world.* New York: Warner Books.

Lewis, M. (1992). Interrupting patriarchy: Politics, resistance and transformation in the feminist classroom. In C. Luke & J. Gore (Eds.), *Feminisms and critical pedagogy* (pp. 167–191). New York: Routledge.

Luke, C. (1992). Feminist politics in radical pedagogy. In C. Luke & J. Gore (Eds.), *Feminisms and critical pedagogy* (pp. 25–53). New York: Routledge.

Lynch, T. (1993). Questions in lectures: Opportunities or obstacles? *Edinburgh Working Papers in Applied Linguistics, 4,* 87–95.

Macmillan, M. (1971a). Recent research for special English courses. *Proceedings of conference on adult English for national development* (pp. 49–53). Beirut: Center for English Language Research and Teaching, the American University of Beirut. (ERIC Document Reproduction Service No. ED 130 525).

Macmillan, M. (1971b). Teaching English to scientists of other languages: Sense or sensibility? *Science and technology in a second language* (pp. 19–30). CILT Report 7. London: Center for Information on Language and Teaching. (ERIC Document Reproduction Service No. ED 063813).

Mahala, D. (1991). Writing utopias: Writing across the curriculum and the promise of reform. *College English, 53,* 773–789.

Master, P. (1998). Positive and negative aspects of the dominance of English. *TESOL Quarterly, 32,* 716–725.

Mathabane, M. (1989). *Kaffir boy in America.* New York: Collier Books.

Mauranen, A. (1993). Contrastive ESP rhetoric: Metatext in Finnish–English economics texts. *English for Specific Purposes, 12,* 3–22.

Mayher, J., Lester, N., & Pradl, G. (1983). *Learning to write/Writing to learn.* Portsmouth, NH: Boynton/Cook.

McDonough, J. (1986). English for academic purposes: A research base? *English for Specific Purposes, 5,* 17–25.

McLaren, P. L. (1994). Postmodernism and the death of politics. In P. L. McLaren & C. Lankshear (Eds.), *Politics of liberation: Paths from Freire* (pp. 193–215). London: Routledge.

McLeod, S., & Maimon, E. (2000). Clearing the air: WAC myths and realities. *College English, 62,* 573–583.

Moll, L. (1989). Teaching second language students: A Vygotskian perspective. In D. M. Johnson & D. H. Roen (Eds.), *Richness in writing: Empowering ESL students* (pp. 55–69). White Plains, NY: Longman.

Morgan, B. D. (1992/3). Teaching the Gulf War in an ESL classroom. *TESOL Journal, 2,* 13–17.

Morgan, B. D. (1998). *The ESL classroom: Teaching, critical practice, and community development.* Toronto: University of Toronto Press.

Moriarty, P. (1998). Learning to be legal: Unintended meanings for adult schools. In T. Smoke (Ed.), *Adult ESL: Politics, pedagogy, and participation in classrooms and community programs* (pp. 17–39). Mahwah, NJ: Lawrence Erlbaum Associates.

Munby, J. (1978). *Communicative syllabus design.* Cambridge, England: Cambridge University Press.

Murray, D. M. (1969). Finding your own voice in an age of dissent. *College Composition and Communication, 20,* 118–123.

Myers, G. (1990). *Writing biology: Texts in the social construction of scientific knowledge.* Madison: University of Wisconsin Press.

Nelson, C. (1999). Sexual identities in ESL: Queer theory and classroom inquiry. *TESOL Quarterly, 33,* 371–391.

Nelson, M. W. (1991). *At the point of need: Teaching basic and ESL writers.* Portsmouth, NH: Boynton/Cook Heinemann.

Oakes, J. (1985). *Keeping track: How schools structure in equality.* New Haven: Yale University Press.

Ortiz, R. (1996). *The 1995–96 coordinated freshman program linked courses project report.* College of Staten Island, City University of New York.

Ortiz, R. (1997). *The 1996–97 coordinated freshman program linked courses project report.* College of Staten Island, City University of New York.

Ostler, S. E. (1980). A survey of academic needs for advanced ESL. *TESOL Quarterly, 14,* 489–502.

Otheguy, R. (1999). *Keeping daylight savings in ESL standards time.* Keynote address at the 26th annual CUNY ESL Council Conference, Hostos Community College, Bronx, NY.

Peirce, B. N. (1995). The theory of methodology in qualitative research. *TESOL Quarterly, 29,* 569–576.

Pennycook, A. (1994). *The cultural politics of English as an international language.* London: Longman.

Pennycook, A. (1997). Vulgar pragmatism, critical pragmatism, and EAP. *English for Specific Purposes, 16,* 253–269.

Pennycook, A. (1999). Introduction: Critical approaches to TESOL. *TESOL Quarterly, 33,* 329–348.

Phillipson, R. (1992). *Linguistic imperialism.* Oxford: Oxford University Press.

Prior, P. (1991). Contextualizing writing and response in a graduate seminar. *Written Communication, 8,* 267–310.

Prior, P. (1995). Redefining the task: An ethnographic examination of writing and response in graduate seminars. In D. Belcher & G. Braine (Eds.), *Academic writing in a second language: Essays on research and pedagogy* (pp. 47–82). Norwood, NJ: Ablex.

Prior, P. A. (1998). *Writing disciplinarity: A sociohistoric account of literate activity in the academy.* Mahwah, NJ: Lawrence Erlbaum Associates.

Raimes, A. (1985). What unskilled ESL students do as they write: A classroom study of composing. *TESOL Quarterly, 19,* 229–258.

Raimes, A. (1991a). Out of the woods: Emerging traditions in the teaching of writing. *TESOL Quarterly, 25,* 407–430.

Raimes, A. (1991b). Instructional balance: From theories to practices in the teaching of writing. In J. Alatis (Ed.), *Georgetown University round table on language and linguistics* (pp. 238–249). Washington, DC: Georgetown University Press.

Ramanathan, V., & Kaplan, R. (1996a). Audience and voice in current L1 composition texts: Some implications for ESL student writers. *Journal of Second Language Writing, 5,* 21–33.

Ramanathan, V., & Kaplan, R. (1996b). Some problematic "channels" in the teaching of critical thinking in current L1 composition textbooks: Implications for L2 student-writers. *Issues in Applied Linguistics, 7,* 225–249.

Ramani, E., Chacko, T., Singh, S. J., & Glendinning, E. H. (1988). An ethnographic approach to syllabus design: A case study of the Indian Institute of Science, Bangalore. *English for Specific Purposes, 7*, 81–90.

Reid, J. (1989). English as a second language composition in higher education: The expectations of the academic audience. In D. M. Johnson & D. H. Roen (Eds.), *Richness in writing: Empowering ESL students* (pp. 220–234). New York: Longman.

Richterich, R., & Chancerel, J. L. (1977). *Identifying the needs of adults learning English as a foreign language.* Oxford: Pergamon.

Robbins, R. H. (1997). *Cultural anthropology: A problem-based approach.* (2nd ed.). Itasca, IL: Peacock Publishers.

Robinson, P. (1980). *ESP (English for specific purposes): The present position.* Oxford: Pergamon Press.

Robinson, P. (1991). *ESP today: A practitioner's guide.* New York: Prentice-Hall.

Santos, T. (1992). Ideology in composition: L¹ and ESL. *Journal of Second Language Writing, 1*, 1–15.

Santos, T. (1998). *The place of politics in second language writing.* Paper presented at the Symposium on Second Language Writing. Purdue University, September, 1998.

Santos, T. (in press). The place of politics in second language writing. In T. Silva & P. K. Matsuda (Eds.), *On second language writing.* Mahwah NJ: Lawrence Erlbaum Associates,.

Saudis reportedly map changes for Aramco. (1988, May 10). *The New York Times*, p. D2.

Selinker, L., Todd-Trimble, M., & Trimble, L. (1978). Rhetorical shifts in EST discourse. *TESOL Quarterly, 12*, 311–320.

Shor, I., & Freire, P. (1987). *A pedagogy for liberation: Dialogues on transforming education.* New York: Bergin & Garvey.

Simon, R. I. (1992). *Teaching against the grain: Texts for a pedagogy of possibility.* New York: Bergin & Garvey.

Smoke, T. (1994). Writing as a means of learning. *College ESL, 4*, 1–11.

Smoke, T. (1998). Critical multiculturalism as a means of promoting social activism and awareness. In T. Smoke (Ed.), *Adult ESL: Politics, pedagogy, and participation in classroom and community programs* (pp. 89–98). Mahwah, NJ: Lawrence Erlbaum Associates.

Spack, R. (1988). Initiating students into the academic discourse community: How far should we go? *TESOL Quarterly, 22*, 29–51.

Spack, R. (1997). The acquisition of academic literacy in a second language: A longitudinal case study. *Written Communication, 14*, 3–26.

Starfield, S. (1990). Science and language: A new look at some old issues. *South African Journal of Higher Education, 4*, 84–89.

Sternglass, M. S. (1997). *Time to know them: A longitudinal study of writing and learning at the college level.* Mahwah, NJ: Lawrence Erlbaum Associates.

Strevens, P. (1971a). English for special purposes: A specialist's viewpoint. *Proceedings of conference on adult English for national development* (pp. 33–48). Beirut: Center for English Language Research and Teaching, the American University of Beirut. (ERIC Document Reproduction Service No. ED 130 525).

Strevens, P. (1971b). Alternatives to daffodils. *Science and technology in a second language* (pp. 7–11). CILT Report 7. London: Center for Information on Language and Teaching. (ERIC Document Reproduction Service No. ED 063813).

Strevens, P. (1977). *New orientations in the teaching of English.* Oxford: Oxford University Press.

Sullivan, E. (1998, April). WBAI, Pacifica Radio.

Swales, J. (1977). ESP in the middle east. In S. Holden (Ed.), *English for specific purposes* (pp. 36–38). London: Modern English Publications.

Swales, J. (1988). *Episodes in ESP: A resource and reference book on the development of English for science and technology.* Hemel Hempstead England: Prentice-Hall International.

Swales, J. (1989). Service English program design and opportunity cost. In R. K. Johnson (Ed.), *The second language curriculum* (pp. 79–90). Cambridge, England: Cambridge University Press.

Swales, J. (1990). *Genre analysis: English in academic and research settings.* Cambridge, England: Cambridge University Press.

Swales, J. (1994). From the editors: From John M. Swales. *English for Specific Purposes, 13,* 200–203.

Tattersal, I. (1995). *The fossil trail: How we know what we think we know about human evolution.* New York: Oxford University Press.

Torbe, M., & Medway, P. (1981). *The climate for learning.* Montclair, NJ: Boynton/Cook Publishers.

Vandrick, S. (1995). Privileged ESL university students. *TESOL Quarterly, 29,* 375–380.

Weiler, K. (1994). Freire and a feminist pedagogy of difference. In P. L. McLaren & C. Lankshear (Eds.), *Politics of liberation: Paths from Freire* (pp. 12–40). London: Routledge.

Wink, J. (1997). *Critical pedagogy: Notes from the real world.* White Plains, NY: Longman.

Zamel, V. (1976). Teaching composition in the ESL classroom: What can we learn from research in the teaching of English? *TESOL Quarterly, 10,* 67–76.

Zamel, V. (1982). Writing: The process of discovering meaning. *TESOL Quarterly, 16,* 195–209.

Zamel, V. (1993). Questioning academic discourse. *College ESL, 3,* 28–39.

Zamel, V. (1995). Strangers in academia: The experiences of faculty and ESL students across the curriculum. *College Composition and Communication, 46,* 506–521.

AUTHOR INDEX

SUBJECT INDEX

CPSIA information can be obtained at www.ICGtesting.com
Printed in the USA
LVOW06s2136040915

452673LV00010B/64/P

9 780805 834345